FAIN[?] PURSUING

Experiences of a young missionary family who went to Bolivia, South America in the early days of New Tribes Mission

The Gess Family in 1952

K. Joyce Gess

FAINT YET PURSUING

K. Joyce Gess

ISBN 1-57502-241-9

Printed in the USA by

MORRIS
PUBLISHING

3212 E. Hwy 30
Kearney, NE 68847
800-650-7888

Dedication

To, our four children
Paul, Ruth, David, and Priscilla
and their families

and

In memory of the faithful, loving husband
God gave me and whom our children
called Daddy

Acknowledgements

My sincere thanks to all those who had a part in bringing this book to fruition by your prayers, encouragement–to keep writing. Especially to Jean Johnson, with her help and advice in so many ways when the project was started.

A word of real appreciation to Wanda Jones, Elnora Nelson and Jack Butler, retired from foreign service and also residents of New Tribes Mission Homes, for the time and effort they spent in proof-reading.

To all those donors and friends who gave and prayed that we might remain in Bolivia for twenty-three years. It was all because of God's faithfulness.

Foreword

In the middle 1960's, a Day of Prayer was being held at a camp site in Michigan, for a group of career and college age people. Myron Gess, a missionary with New Tribes Mission, home on furlough from Bolivia, was our missionary speaker.

In 1972, I met Myron again, along with his lovely wife Joy, but this time was a little different. Here we were all serving as staff members at New Tribes Bible Institute in Waukesha, Wisconsin. I was one of those young people from the Michigan camp and Myron was one of the teachers.

Myron and Joy always impressed me with their love and service for the Lord and others. In 1979, Myron and Joy retired, due to Myron's health problems. I had the privilege of helping them move over to Michigan, where Joy lovingly cared for Myron until his home going in 1986!

Then in 1990 I met Joy again at our New Tribes Mission Retirement Center in Sanford, Florida. We were on staff together once again. In 1993 Joy retired and soon had a desire from the Lord to share Myron's life long Journals in book form to be called, "Faint Yet Pursuing."

I'm sure the heart beat of the Gesses' service for the Lord will be evident and will challenge you to keep pursuing when you feel faint in your Christian life and walk with the Lord.

"And let us not be weary in well doing:
for in due season we shall reap, if we faint not."
Galatians 6:9

Don Seiling
New Tribes Missionary

Table of Contents

How It All Began

Chapter 1

Myron Lyle Gess was born and raised on a fruit farm in lower Michigan. His parents had immigrated from Germany. They were not a Christian family and never went to church. It was in his senior year of high school through the influence of a Christian buddy that he came to know the Lord as his Savior.

Soon after this he committed his life to the Lord to be used in whatever way the Lord would lead. He entered Moody Bible Institute in 1940.

§ § §

Kathleen Joyce Ford, was born in Port Perry, Ontario, Canada. Her parents were both Christians and she came to know the Lord at an early age, but didn't come to the assurance of her salvation until she was twelve years old. From the time she started school, friends always seemed to call her "Joy", instead of Joyce. This nickname has stayed with her down through the years and very few people know her as Joyce.

§ § §

A friend and Joy traveled from our home in Ottawa, Ontario to study at the Moody Bible Institute in Chicago. It was quite an experience for two young ladies who had never journeyed that far away from home alone. It was the fall of 1941.

Soon after we began our first semester, a social was announced as a welcome to new students. The freshmen were to wear name tags. The advanced classes were there to welcome us. During the course of the evening I met Myron. Unknown to me he copied my name on a little piece of paper. That was the beginning of a life-time marriage, love and friendship.

We were married in my home church in Ottawa, Ontario in 1943. A beautiful reception was held in the backyard rock garden of my home. Together we recommitted our lives to the Lord for His service.

The foreign field was always uppermost in both of our hearts. We didn't have too much knowledge of those "foreign fields", but applied to two different Mission boards. We were rejected however, and were told that Myron was just too thin, and wouldn't have the health to stay and work on foreign soil.

How subtle the enemy is in trying to discourage one from walking in the path God sets before him.

An interesting incident happened about this time. A former roommate of Myron's there in Moody Bible Institute was very careless about his study hours and consequently didn't make the grade he needed for ending the school year. He dropped out of day school and the same thing happened when he entered evening school. He was not serious about his studies and spent most of his hours just wasting his time. A year or so later, Myron met this fellow once again. In the course of conversation, Myron had told him about being rejected for foreign service. His reply was "Oh, come over to New Tribes Mission, they take anyone!" As we talked the matter over later, Myron said to me, "If they took that fellow, I don't want anything to do with that Mission!"

§ § §

As newlyweds, we began our ministry in the Clarksville Bible Church, but always felt drawn to other missionary type work.

We were later accepted as missionaries with the Mission then known as the American Sunday School Union. We felt that this too was missionary work, although not on foreign soil.

The Lord gave opportunities to witness in five different counties. Souls were saved and Sunday Schools established. In one of these Sunday School groups a lady who became a close friend of ours asked if we could have a couple of representatives from New Tribes Mission come to minister in the Sunday School. This was the mother of George Hosback, who was one of the five fellows to give their lives in the initial Ayore contact. We gave our consent.

During these special meetings, Ken Johnston and Jim Ostewig stayed in our home and we traveled together over five different counties.

Once again, we were challenged to press on to the foreign field. We were given encouragement to submit our application to the Mission.

§ § §

How thrilled we were when our letter of acceptance came!

We were building a new home at the time, and were also in debt. In those next few weeks everything was sold except the few things which we planned to take with us. We were out of debt and so thankful to God that HE had made this possible. We vowed from then on to spend money only as the Lord gave it to us. The Lord has honored that decision in many ways.

I will add at this point that we did make inquiries about this "buddy" of Myron's and found that he was never accepted by New Tribes Mission.

About the same time there were two other families challenged to give their lives, and they were accepted by the Mission. They too sold everything. We became very close as a group. We prayed and talked and planned together, and in the summer of 1948 set out to travel together to our Missionary Training Institute in Fouts Springs, California. Perhaps we looked like a group of migrants as we traveled -- three cars, three trailers, three tents, and two-burner Coleman stoves. There were eight children and six adults in all. We cooked our meals along the way, and slept in our tents at night.

One afternoon as we were traveling through the desert, the back wheel from our trailer came off, bounced on the back of the car, over the roof and down on the hood of the car. Then it kept on rolling down the road in front of us.

Perhaps we weren't going fast enough for that wheel, but we knew one thing: that was that God was protecting us. No one was hurt.

We had been asked to come to a camp in the Mendocino forest which had been purchased for a possible "second" camp.

Our days in Mendocino were not easy, but God has not always promised an easy road. Every day was a rainy one, and there were always wet, cold drops of rain falling from the trees. We seldom saw sunshine. We had three children then with another baby on the way.

Our youngest, two year old David, was sick with asthma most of the time and grew worse each time we left the cabin. I was pretty much cabin bound and not able to attend many of the classes. How our thoughts churned and churned. Would we still be accepted by the Mission if we didn't attend those classes? How good and faithful the Lord was in those days to keep our eyes on Him, and keep pressing towards the field before us.

In January of 1949 we left Mendocino and entered the Fouts Springs Boot Camp. Mendocino camp was closed again soon after that time. Will we ever forget that one lane, winding road leading into camp? Our times in Fouts Springs were precious times, learning to live with one another, work and play and pray together.

One thing that stands out in my mind--so vividly--is the time we spent together as a group, fellowshipping, studying the Word and praying together in what we called "Cloud Club". There were joys and sorrows, struggles and trials and victories, shared and prayed over. We went forth with new determination to press on.

How encouraged we were when one day we were approached by a Mission representative, and asked if we thought we could be ready to go on the first trip of the mission plane in June? GOD WAS TO PERFORM A MIRACLE!

Moving Out

Chapter 2

"There goes old Noah building his ark!" That was the comment I overheard another fellow give to Myron on a sunny afternoon in Fouts Springs.

Time was at a premium. We had been asked if we could be ready to go on the first trip of our mission plane going to Bolivia. After much prayer we felt the Lord leading that way, even though we had no money whatsoever towards fare. Was that a problem? I didn't think so nor did Myron. If the Lord wanted us on the plane HE would provide. So we were making preparations.

Myron was outside using some lumber which had been available in the camp to make shipping boxes. We would have to ship our belongings separately, and take only what was necessary on the plane. It seemed as if the whole camp was praying for the Lord's guidance for us. We continued to make preparations, so when this remark about being like "Old Noah" came to Myron, his reply was, "Yes, that's right, and did you notice that it is just starting to rain?"

After so many years of training and feeling the Lord would have us on a foreign field serving Him, it hardly seemed possible that we were really on our way.

We were to leave Fouts Springs for Chico where we would board the plane and begin the trip across the States. Several stops were made where we held special meetings in different churches. Then we crossed the Pacific to South America.

"Will you please come and have breakfast with us before you leave?" The invitation came from Carl and Cora Taylor, some dear friends of ours who were also preparing for the field.

"Oh yes, that would be wonderful," I replied, "then we can get all our last minute things packed."

We had three children, Paul was not quite five years old. Ruth was four, David, two, and I was expecting our fourth little one to make his or her appearance in October. June would be a good time to travel.

The day arrived. We were all packed and ready to drive to Chico where we would leave our car with the family who had purchased it. Early in the morning we were served a delicious breakfast. During the course of conversation, Carl said to Myron, "Cora and I were just wondering if you had all of your passage money and enough to carry with you on the trip." Myron and I looked at one another, for we knew we didn't; yet, we hesitated to tell others our need. We knew the Lord would provide. Carl asked again, "Would you mind telling us just how much you have for traveling?" Well, at this point, Myorn felt the Lord would have us be honest with the Taylors and share the facts. We had exactly five dollars in our pockets. We had been told by the Mission Committee that we could go as far as Chico, but could not board the plane until the money was there for our fare. Would God still undertake? Or did He plan for us to travel at a later date.

Then the Taylors shared with us that they had deposited enough money in Chico to be applied to our fare. They also gave us additional money for traveling expenses. Tears filled our eyes as we realized once again God's faithfulness in supplying our every need. Through some misunderstanding the Mission had never informed us of this gift.

No, we weren't rich missionaries. Neither did we ever go hungry. We experienced God's continued faithfulness in taking us to Bolivia and keeping us there.

"Ha! Ha! Such a tall, skinny man! He's come to Bolivia only to die!"

"What is he saying?" Myron asked one of the missionaries standing close by. Not wanting to discourage us on our arrival, the reply was, "Oh, he's laughing, I guess he thinks you are pretty tall and thin!"

So this was our welcome to Bolivia as Myron and I and our three children disembarked from our plane. I suppose the curious Bolivians had reasons to speak as they did since they are rather diminutive in stature and Myron was six feet four inches tall and weighed only one hundred and sixty pounds. God kept us there in Bolivia for twenty three more years.

We had had a somewhat arduous but interesting flight from the United States in our Missions' DC-3 named The Tribesman. The purpose of the plane and the missionaries aboard was to reach brown-skinned people who had never heard the gospel of Jesus Christ. With stops in Cuba, Venezuela, Dutch Guiana (now Surinam), and Brazil, we were introduced to many new cultures and climates.

Chapter 2

"I don't believe I remember ever being hotter than I was last evening." This was Myron's comment after we returned from a service held in one of the national churches in Belen, Brazil.

He had been asked to share the Word with the help of an interpreter. The culture demanded that a well-dressed man wear a coat in church or even on the street. All Myron had was a wool suit because that was the only suit he owned. It was in the middle of the hot season, and an extremely warm evening.

Having arrived in Bolivia along with several other new missionaries and also in the company of our founder and leader, Mr. Paul Fleming, it was in order that we have a conference with the missionaries already on the field. Seven years before, five of our men had laid down their lives in an attempt to reach the savage Ayore Indians in the nearby jungle (Not to be confused with the occasion many years later when five other men from other missions lost their lives in Ecuador). A friendly contact was made three years later and now plans must be laid for the future of that work and with many other similar tribes.

"We have made preparations for you and your family to stay in the small building where mission baggage is stored." This was the instruction we had received from our hostess as she was trying to find rooms for all the travelers disembarking from the mission plane.

We knew that there was going to be some doubling up in order to find the room needed. A double bed was set up for Myron and I on the dirt floor. Our three preschoolers slept in hammocks suspended crosswise above us. I don't remember being bothered by mosquitoes because we were more concerned about the rats that scurried below us and sometimes over us.

Nine days later we continued on to Cochabamba, flying at times as high as sixteen thousand feet through passes in the Andes Mountains. We were lightheaded and nauseated in our unpressurized plane and our heads seemed as if they would split as we descended to eight thousand five hundred feet and the interesting city of Cochabamba which was to be our home for the next year and a half.

In many respects, Cochabamba, Bolivia, is a lovely place to live--after your body has adjusted to the eight thousand five hundred foot elevation. It's climate is considered one of the best in the world. Fruits, vegetables and flowers are in abundance. Accentuating this are the Quechua Indian women with their colorful full skirts and tall white hats. Many Aymara Indians were also seen in the market places of Cochabamba. The ladies were dressed almost like the Quechuas, with the exception of their hats being more like wool fedoras.

Streets are swept by hand before dawn each morning, but ignore, if you can, the odor of human excrement in the open sewers along the streets and roadside.

A formal course in the Spanish language was not to be our privilege. Instead we were to work language study into our schedule as best we could with older missionaries and a Bolivian university student as our tutors. Oh the blunders we made in those first days.

I remember one occasion in particular. Myron had volunteered for the job of buyer and bookkeeper for the Bolivian field. I was to be the hostess of our mission guest house which was also our home. One Saturday morning in those early days, the Quechua cook we had at that time to help in the kitchen went with me to market. I had wanted to get some meat. Oh, yes, I knew how to ask that. "Please sell me some 'jabon'," I said to the little Quechua lady there in the market. Can you imagine my chagrin when she handed piece of soap instead of the ham which I thought I was ordering? The Spanish word for ham is "jamon" instead of "jabon". There were many other trying moments in our language learning. Imagine if you can, our trying to make purchases, secure the release of shipments from customs or give instructions to a couple of hired girls when we could speak only a smattering of Spanish and that only in the present tense! We were forced to learn and to learn quickly.

As it was our first assignment to serve in this way, there were many lessons to be learned. The days were long, but we found the Lord's grace and strength always sufficient. We always appreciated those experiences which came our way and brought a good laugh.

One particular order came from a dear co-worker who had been on the field for many years. She wrote:

"Myron, when I was in Cochabamba a few weeks ago, I happened to see in one of the store windows -- just about a block from the plaza -- I'm not sure which direction -- a pair of bloomers. I guess I should have purchased them when I saw them, but since I returned home I felt I really need them. Would you go to 'that store' and purchase them?"

In the same letter came this request:

"Oh yes, and Myron, I want to make a suit. I saw one in another store window which I would like to have made. I don't know how much material it would take. Ask Joy, she will know! Plenty long enough to sit on! Then you know the color -- whichever color would suit me best. Well, Myron, you buy and I'll PRAY!"

Cochabamba

Chapter 3

The country of Bolivia seems to be well-known for it's revolutions. This is always an interesting time when foreigners, especially Americans, usually have to keep to their homes and avoid going out on the street.

On one particular weekend, we were expecting our Mission plane to arrive soon with another load of missionaries from the United States. How we rejoiced to see more help coming into Bolivia to fill the gaps where laborers were so badly needed. We knew we would have to get food supplies in before the plane arrived -- then a State of Siege was declared!

Myron said he would help me, by going with another missionary to a large open market to buy a quantity of potatoes. In the meantime, I took our cook, and went to a smaller market nearer home to buy vegetables and meat if we could find it. We had just gotten our basket filled, when the shooting began.

"Run, Senora, run!" our little cook shouted. My response was, "You run with the basket, I can't!" You see Priscilla, our youngest child was due to be born any day.

And was Myron able to get the potatoes? It was impossible to drive the pickup when the firing began, so Myron and his companion retreated to the safety of our friend's garage. After unloading the potatoes in the garage, he picked his way home on foot over a very circuitous route. Shots were being fired all around. However, we knew the Lord's protection and eventually we were all safely home.

We were warned by radio that at night the city would be bombed. Many took refuge in the mountains surrounding the city, but we stayed in our home. However, before going to bed that night, I laid out clothes for the children. Myron gathered together important papers and the mission funds, just in case we would have to leave and take refuge elsewhere. Before the night passed, bombs did fall. One demolished a building only about four blocks from us. The concussion cracked windows in our house but we were kept safe. Psalms 91:1 "He that dwelleth in the secret place of the Most High shall abide under the shadow of the Almighty." Psalms 63:7: "Because thou hast been my help, therefore, in the shadow of thy wings will I rejoice."

During the following day, when it was still too dangerous to attempt to do any business in town, we were all sitting around the dinner table when a plane flew overhead. Paul, our eldest, and always interested in planes, went to the door to look. "Daddy, Mommy, it's our TRIBESMAN PLANE!" Daddy's reply was, "I don't think so Paul, they wouldn't be allowed to land at a time like this!" The incident was almost forgotten. Dinner was over, and the maids began to take care of cleaning up the dishes, when there was a loud knock on the door. Our cook went to the door to see who it might be at a time like this. She opened the door rather gingerly, let out a squeal of surprise, and then said, "Senora, Americanos!" The plane had arrived indeed, and Paul was correct in his announcement. How glad we were for the basket of vegetables.

Just three weeks later, on a busy October afternoon, a bright healthy little girl decided to make her appearance. We named her Priscilla Joy. In those days in Bolivian hospitals one could not expect to have expert nursing care and especially at night when the nurses slept like everyone else. During that first night, I was thankful that Priscilla was in a crib in the same room as mine when she needed attention. Oh, yes, she didn't cost us as much as if we had been in the United States. Hospital and Doctor charges came to forty five dollars!

Our Mission in those days was a fast-growing organization. Every few weeks the Mission plane brought another load of missionaries and this meant that we had more guests at the Mission home. In an attempt to keep pace, we moved twice to larger quarters in a year and a half. The last place was a three bedroom house with a smaller guest house behind it. This was fairly adequate until the tile and mud roof of the guest room caved in and we had to accommodate sixteen people in the main house alone! Once there were thirty-six people for a meal. It had to be buffet style!

In spite of all the ministries in the physical and material realm that took most of our time and attention, we took advantage of opportunities to make Christ known to the Bolivian people. For example, on Sunday afternoons, a few of us would take a spring-operated phonograph and gospel records to a place where people would be apt to gather. We would then pass out tracts and witness even if it were in faulty Spanish. A few professed to accept Christ as Saviour.

Here, too, the enemy was at work and sought to discourage. One Sunday afternoon in particular, the group from the Mission was standing around a big tree in the center of the plaza holding a meeting. Don and Lyda Slife were standing on the outer edge of the circle when all of a sudden, a speeding car came by and hit Lyda, knocking her down. Her leg was severely injured, resulting in surgery and amputation. We were all shaken by this event, but praised the Lord that no lives were lost. Psalms 91:4,5, "He shall cover thee with his feathers, and under his wings shalt thou trust; his truth shall be thy shield and buckler."

"Thou shalt not be afraid for the terror by night or the arrow that flieth by day......for He shall give his angels charge over thee, to keep thee in all thy ways."

That Christmas, with gifts we were given by friends, we were able to buy a small shortwave radio.

What a thrill it was to hear a news broadcast in English from the Voice of America or the British Broadcasting Company! But one evening---I shall never forget it---this little radio brought us the heart-rending news that our Mission plane on it's eighth flight to South America, had struck a mountain in Venezuela killing all aboard! We sat stunned! Yet, this was only the first time God was going to allow us, as a mission, to be put to such a severe test. A second plane was to crash soon after that in Wyoming, killing our founder and director, Paul Fleming. Truly, if New Tribes Mission had not been of God, it would have folded up at that time, but the fire of trials were used to purify the hearts and intensify the zeal of those who remained. Lives were challenged and the Mission continued to grow.

Adjusting to a new climate and culture plus trying to learn a new language is always difficult. Being thrust into a ministry almost immediately upon arrival in Bolivia, in addition, took a toll on our health and strength. I began to lose weight excessively and Myron was often sick with one thing or another so our co-workers suggested a rest. We flew to the capital city of LaPaz to spend a few days while Myron at the same time could transact some Mission business. Before our stay was finished, I became very ill from the effects of the high elevation and it was necessary to call a doctor to our hotel. Incidentally, the airport of LaPaz at an elevation of thirteen thousand five hundred feet, is the highest commercial airport in the world. Later, fellow missionaries took over our responsibilities so that we might visit the lowlands of Bolivia to see if life at a lower altitude would help me. We made these trips at separate times. I went to visit in the city of

Santa Cruz at the foot of the Andes Mountains where we also have a mission home. Myron traveled farther east by train almost to the Brazilian border. It was here some of our missionaries were working with the Ayore Indians who had killed five of our earlier missionaries.

In Myron's journal he tells about that trip: "One could fly to Santa Cruz on an American airline but from there travel was by a narrow gauge Brazilian train made up of box cars, flat cars and cattle cars, pulled by a tiny wood-burning locomotive. The passenger cars were box cars with a board seat along the walls. Since on this particular occasion the passenger cars were completely filled, I looked for another place to ride. A flat car was not the best choice because of the hot sun and the sparks from the locomotive. Also there was no protection from a possible rain. I noticed that the steers in a certain cattle car were tied at a forty-five degree angle and there was a clean place in one of the corners. It was there I rode, rather comfortably, all one night, the steers were not bothering me nor I the steers!"

We were grateful for our few days of rest away from our responsibilities and upon returning to Cochabamba took up our work with renewed enthusiasm and vigor. The vigor didn't continue, however, for before long Myron was down in bed with a high fever and an aching body with malaria he had picked up in the lowlands. He was to feel the effects of this for several years in spite of the medication which was given him. In those days there didn't seem to be a good cure available.

With the crash of our second mission plane and the death of our founder and director, Paul Fleming, a shift in personnel was necessary. Our field chairman was asked to return to the states but before he left Myron suggested that he be on the lookout for replacements for us in the Cochabamba work. If the Lord provided, then we would try life on a more permanent basis at a lower altitude. My body did not seem to be adjusting to the higher altitude. Also, our hearts were constantly drawn to the Indian tribal work.

The New Cook

Chapter 4

There she was at the front gate of the mission home. A short, stocky, Quechua Indian lady. She had come at the advice of her cousin who was already working for the "foreigners".

What a beautiful sight she was. Not that we were overly anxious to hire another cook, taking the place of the one who just left us, but she was clean, well dressed in her Quechua outfit of startling bright colors. Many petticoats under her heavy, wool skirt created a real dirndl appearance. A lovely brightly colored, hand woven shawl of pure llama wool covered her shoulders. She wore a lovely cotton blouse, with layered ripples of lace peeking out from under her shawl. Almost hidden by all the layers of skirts were the handmade sandals she wore. These were made from used car tires. They were made to endure!

Eduvijes, for that was her Quechua name, was a friendly person. She was very eager to learn "our way of cooking" but she wanted to please those for whom she worked. It was my job to teach her how to cook some of our American dishes, and how to follow a recipe, but how we all enjoyed those tasty Bolivian dishes she served us as well.

Eduvijes had long, black hair, woven into two long braids down her back. Her shiny, bronze skin almost glistened at times. Not too many days went by without the sound of her singing at her work. Her hands were roughened and calloused by hard farm work on the hillside of the Andes Mountains, but they were always kept clean. Her dark brown eyes sparkled as she spoke.

It was also my privilege to have devotions with our three maids whom the Mission home employed. I shall always remember the day when Eduvijes came to know the Lord, and the joy she expressed when she came to the assurance that God loved her and died for her. If she was happy before that day, she radiated peace and joy even more when she came to know her Saviour.

With years, come changes however. We were moving out of the city to a remote village. Eduvijes wanted to come with us. The Indian work was heavy upon our hearts. We had been advised, because of health reasons, not to make a move suddenly from the higher altitude to the lowlands. About this same time, we had been told of a village called Samaipata on the highway between Cochabamba and Santa Cruz, which had no missionary. It was a healthy climate with an altitude of five thousand feet.

The Lord seemed to direct us to go there. We were rather overwhelmed by the way the Lord provided through gifts of money from fellow missionaries to help pay our moving and travel expenses.

We had hesitated when Eduvijes asked to move out with us. For one thing she was a valuable worker at the Mission home. However, she had the desire to witness, and we knew that she would be a real help to us in so many ways. After praying much about the matter, we said she could go. We knew it would be a real adjustment on her part as well -- not knowing quite what was ahead of us.

In addition to our family of six,-- there was Eduvijes and her daughter, a little girl just the same age as our Ruth. Paul was having some physical problems at this time, so we had decided to keep both Paul and Ruth home for one year and I would teach them.

We first flew to the lowland city of Santa Cruz, and the children, Eduvijes and I would remain there while Myron made the trip back up the mountain road by truck. He would look for a place for us to live.

It was a moonlit night but not an easy trip riding atop a load of lumber. Myron writes: "At times a sheer wall of rock rose up on one side while on the other side one looked straight down to a rushing river several hundred feet below. All in all it was a bit scary since the highway was only a one laned dirt road carved out of the mountain side. The people of the village were friendly, but cautious since we were evangelicals, and they were of a different "religious persuasion." To be too friendly would invoke persecution from their neighbors. To rent us a house was an even more serious matter but one woman was willing to risk it.

"How much would the rent be?" Myron asked.

"Well, for you I would have to have a little more because I'm taking rather a risk in allowing you and your family to live here." She also felt that because we were the so-called 'rich Americans' she could charge a little more and make a profit.

The house -- more literally an apartment -- was on the main plaza, and although noisy, was ideally located for contact with the people.

When Myron got back to Santa Cruz, we secured the services of a Brazilian missionary and his Dodge power wagon to take us to our new home. I'm sure we resembled a family of migrant workers as we traveled. Our two girls and I rode in the cab with the driver and the rest of the family perched on top of furniture and baggage. The road was extremely rough and Ruth was sick with a very bad sore throat and high fever. If we had the desire to choose which day we would travel we would have postponed it for a couple of days, but that wasn't to be.

At one point when travel was especially hard, Ruth looked up into my face and said, "Mommy, we're doing this for Jesus' sake, aren't we?" Ruth was six years old then, but now as a missionary in her own right, travels over similar roads with her husband and family to reach the un-reached of Bolivia for Christ.

Since there were already a couple of Christian families in the area, we had a start toward a Sunday School and Bible study. However, to have peaceful gatherings, as is our privilege in the United States, was a different thing. The leaders of the more popular and official religion of Bolivia would deliberately pass by our house during a meeting to spy out who was in attendance so that they might bring pressure on them to discontinue coming. Also, they stirred up the children and young people of the village to shout and yell outside our door, throwing sticks and small stones inside while a meeting was in progress.

One day, in conversation with the Chief of Police of the village, Myron remarked, "I understand that the constitution of Bolivia is supposed to grant liberty to all religious groups." After that conversation, all was quiet during the meetings.

Since our objective was to reach the country people as well as the villagers with the gospel, Myron often made visits to their homes. On one occasion he traveled some distance on horseback with an Arab merchant from our village. He was a professing Christian. An uncle of his was ill and the town doctor had prescribed some injections for him. Myron was asked to accompany this friend to administer the injections which were needed.

More from Myron's Journal: "The uncle was of a Moslem belief. The house was small and several members of the family slept in the same room. I was glad when they moved a bed for me to the front porch where there was more ventilation. My pillow was covered with a man's shirt to serve as a pillow case. Fresh warm goat's milk was served. It tasted good! My first meal consisted of what appeared to be shell macaroni. It turned out to be tripe, the cooked lining of the cow's stomach. It had spoiled in the hot weather, and one could hardly stand it's taste. What's more, I was seated with the Arab at a small table near the sick uncle who watched every move "the gringo" or foreigner made. In order not to offend, I found that by putting the food far back on my tongue, missing the taste buds, I was able to swallow a few spoonfuls. Finally, my friend also found the food distasteful, and asked to have it taken away."

On another trip into the moutain area my hubby spent the night in the country home of a humble Christian family. They gave him a bed which was literally a platform of adobe blocks extending from the wall. The "mattress" was a pad of homespun wool. The dogs and pigs had free roam of the house. As a result of the animal's freedom, fleas were in abundance. "When I tried to sleep, they covered my whole body." Myron said, "It was only because of the weariness from climbing the mountain paths that sleep came."

"In the morning I made a visit to the bushes, where I removed all my clothing and covered my body with insect repellent. This brought relief."

In reflecting on this experience, Myron wondered if even the patriarch Abraham and his herdsmen had a few fleas in their blankets.

On still another occasion, as he and some Bolivian friends visited another farm family, they were taught how to eat with homemade tableware. In this case, the people were very poor and had carved some new wooden spoons for their use. Lacking meat to serve, they had prepared potatoes and soft boiled eggs. How did a person get the egg out of it's shell with such a large wooden spoon. Of course these friends had the answer, "Oh, just turn the spoon around and use the handle," they said. It worked fine.

In this same home was a teenage boy who came to know the Lord as his Savior. Unknown to Myron he was a leper. Little did we realize that he would become a patient in the leprosarium in which we were to work several years later. After some time the disease was arrested, and he became a pastor of a national church.

As we reflect on our several month's stay in the village of Samaipata, we recall a couple of incidents that indicated we were still "gringos" with a lot to learn concerning the customs of Bolivia. One was that a man does not carry water from the river for household use. Myron did this after we first arrived and drew smiles from many of the town's people. The water carrying is done by servants or lower class women and is carried on top of their head in a large clay jug. Myron didn't attempt to carry it on his head!

Yard goods as well as many other items were sold in the local shop. One day Eduvijes and I were doing some buying and I saw some bolts of blue and white plaid flannel.

Upon arriving home. I said to Myron, "Wouldn't that material make some nice warm shirts for you?" "It seems as if it would be fine for this cooler mountain weather," he replied. So I bought enough material to make two shirts for him.

Later, we noticed that many women of the town were soon to blossom out in dresses made of the same material!

Another lesson in culture taught us that our friend and companion, Eduvijes, who had come to be with us in the work, being a Quechua Indian from the highlands, was not accepted by the town people. They particularly did not accept her as a teacher of a children's Sunday School class. She was looked down upon when she attempted to witnesses or even visit with the people of the town.

One day, feeling unwanted and out of place, Eduvijes and her little girl returned to the city of Cochabamba and continued working at the Mission home there.

At about this time, Mamie Lahue, the mother of Eleanor Lahue working in the Beni, came to work with us. Mamie came to the field when she was older and had raised her family. She was a tremendous blessing to us and the people loved her too. She rented an apartment a few blocks from us. It was a corner house with a huge back yard. This back yard didn't have any gate and no opening in the fence to enter what was really a small pasture. It was an ideal place to keep our horse, Che. How would we get him into the pasture? Mamie had the answer, "Oh just bring him in the front door, through the house, and out the back into the yard." Not too many people would appreciate escorting a horse through their living room. The plan worked! The hay in the pasture became an ideal diet for Che. It gave a better appearance to what was supposed to be a back yard as well.

We were continuing to have problems in our meetings. Mamie had the answer for this as well, "That's no problem, I'll just stand and guard the door." We hesitated, then Myron said, "What if you get hit with one of those stones?" "Don't even worry," was her reply. "They wouldn't throw a stone at me." And they didn't!

Eduvijes was wise enough to see that Vitalia, her daughter received a good education. She eventually became a nurse. Because she had played with the American children, she also learned to speak English well. She and her mother eventually immigrated to the United States. They now own their home and automobile. Both have learned to drive. They are still our devoted friends and sisters in the Lord.

What about the children of missionaries as they face different cultures and perhaps lack some of the things that a young person in the United States or Canada would have? So many people feel it is unfair to take children to a foreign country and subject them to life on a more primitive plane. Our observations were that children adapt much more quickly and easily to language and culture than adults and are often used of the Lord to gain an entrance into hearts and homes long before the missionary has won a friendship. Our youngest child, Priscilla, who was just a toddler, had long blonde hair and blue eyes. She was an especially effective icebreaker, even with those who most zealously opposed us and the gospel.

As time went on, and our health improved, we felt that we should be more directly involved in the main thrust of New Tribes Mission, that of reaching tribal people with the Word of God. In an area of jungle country northeast of the city of Santa Cruz was a group of Ayore Indians who were making attacks on a ranch called Las Pocitas and a village named Madrecitas. These Indians were savage and believed to be a splinter group of the tribe that had killed five of our missionaries nine years earlier. We decided that we would look to the Lord to be able to move out into this area and attempt to establish a friendship with these Indians.

Our first step was to return to Santa Cruz once again with our household belongings. We still had our big white horse named "Che" or "Pal". A Bolivian business man who owned a large truck carried us and our household goods with no difficulty. He would have hauled Che too but Che had other ideas and refused to board the truck and had to be ridden to Santa Cruz.

Although our move from Samaipata was made in January, it was not until early April that we were able to continue on to the village of Madrecitas. November thru February are the rainy, hot summer months in Bolivia. Travel on jungle roads is next to impossible. Our time of waiting, however, was occupied to good advantage. Myron was able to lend a hand in the construction of our new school for missionary children. We were also able to attend field conference as a family. What blessings came to us each day as we fellowshipped together around the Word, sharing our hearts, telling how the Lord was working. What a rich time!

A Surprise Encounter

Chapter 5

We were moving from our mountain village to the lowlands. The two younger children were still at home while the two eldest children were in our Mission school. Our hearts were with the tribal work, and rumors were that another part of the savage Indian tribe of Ayores had been sighted in the area of a small ranching settlement called Madrecitas in the lowlands.

It was necessary for Myron to go ahead to see if a house was available to rent or if one would have to be built. The children and I would wait at our Santa Cruz Mission home. It was a three day trip by horseback. A dear friend and coworker, Bob Bodin, accompanied Myron on the trip. Bob and Emily Bodin were in charge of the mission home in Santa Cruz. While I was waiting with the children, Emily and I had such good times of fellowship. I was able to help in many of their daily responsibilities as well.

The two men started out on horseback. It was tiring and difficult because Myron hadn't been used to riding such a long distance. At one point, the men decided to let their horses drink from a small water hole along the trail. "It's not necessary to dismount," Bob said to Myron, "let's just bring the horses to the edge of the pond."

Myron had some reservations about such a move, but did agree. His horse had no sooner gotten to the edge of the water when it lost it's footing. Myron was thrown over his horse's head and into the water. The water was not deep--but there was enough to require him to change his clothing. The extra clothing in his saddlebag didn't get wet. He was in the process of stripping his wet clothes off when to his surprise he heard,

"Buenas Dias Senor." Out from nowhere had come a lady to the pond to do her washing. She thought it wonderful to have someone to talk with and wasn't in the least bit of a hurry to leave. It didn't seem to bother her in the least that Myron was only half dressed. Bob got a real laugh out of the situation and was still chuckling as they continued on. Bob remarked to Myron, "Just to see your face as you stood there, Myron, with such a shocked expression was more than I could handle without a good laugh." The trip continued without further incident except to laugh together as they reminisced over the surprise encounter.

§ § §

MADRECITAS

The village of Madrecitas consisted primarily of a ranch house and store owned and operated by a German enterprise and the Bolivians who worked for this corporation. There was, in addition, an older German man who was a landowner. He had married a Bolivian woman who had borne him several children. Two of his sons were prominent in the community. It was this German-Bolivian family that agreed to rent us a new, but rather crudely built house on the far side of the village next to the jungle. The house consisted of walls made of split palm bark arranged much like a picket fence with about as many cracks in it. There were only openings where eventually the windows and doors could be hung. The roof was a palm thatch, inhabited by bats, snakes and centipedes and the floor was firmly packed dirt. There was only one room which eventually became a bedroom for both us and the children while the unwalled front porch was used for cooking, eating and receiving visitors. The "palacious" habitation was rented to us only because the owners were afraid to live there. Why? Because a group of yet uncivilized Ayore Indians in the area were making attacks on homes that appeared to be most vulnerable to them.

The men returned to Santa Cruz, and then came the final packing and buying of supplies to move out to this area of Madrecitas. We would need supplies at least for one month. The day came when a truck was hired to take us and our belongings. "Oh yes, I'll be there at the Mission home to load up and be on our way the day after tomorrow," the driver assured us. We were packed and ready, but no truck driver showed up. Bolivia is the land of "manana" or "tomorrow".

There were three more useless attempts to find out when our truck would arrive. Finally it showed up at the time we least expected it to come -- about five o'clock in the afternoon.

It's one thing to take a plane or train or other public transportation in the United States that late in the day, but it is another thing in Bolivia. We didn't dare indicate that we would have rather waited until morning. By about eight o'clock that night we were finally on the way. We carried lots of boiled water with us -- there were no ice cubes!

Riding on top of such a load isn't very conducive to sleep either. The two children and I were given opportunity to ride in the cab of the truck. It was still very crowded and not a lot of room to move around. Early the next morning we came to a ranch called Las Positas. We put our sleeping bags on the ground and stayed there for the rest of the night. The next day would bring another type of transportation. All of our belongings were unloaded from the truck on the banks of the Rio Grande, or Grand River. In what appeared to us to be no more than a dugout canoe, we were to cross the wide Grand River in this way. Several trips were made and finally everything was on the other side of the river. There would be just seven and one half miles on the other side of the river before we were to reach the village of Madrecitas which would become home to us. It surely wouldn't take too long and we would still have time to unpack what was needed for the night.

Another truck was waiting and once again everything was loaded and we started on our way. The so-called "road" didn't appear much more than a muddy trail to us. There were unexpected mud holes where the truck would be stuck and had to be pulled out. Then one of the tie rods broke, something else went wrong, and the driver informed us that we would have to wait there -- in the middle of that jungle area -- until they could return by foot to the ranch by the river for truck parts. We waited! The mosquitos were fierce, so we unpacked the two jungle hammocks for the children so they would be a little more protected. Once the truck was repaired we were once again on our way. That last seven and one half miles took thirty six hours before we finally reached our destination. To say we were tired, was putting it rather mildly.

Once the truck was unloaded we attempted to make beds for all of us. We were more than ready, and whatever else needed to be done in getting unpacked would wait until the next day.

We knew that if the Lord could protect us in the time of actual contact with these Indians, He could also protect us during our day to day living. There weren't many precautions we could take, but we did keep a small kerosene lantern burning low throughout the night. All of us New Tribes missionaries had pledged ourselves not to kill an Indian in self-defense.

It was in this situation that we began to get our bearings in our new endeavor. There were many new people to meet and witness to and just living itself took considerable time. All of our water came from a large water hole in the center of a pasture where all the town women also came to wash their clothes. The water we used for drinking and cooking had to be boiled and filtered. The only washing machine we had was one you pumped by hand. We had no refrigerator and our cooking was done over an open wood fire on a raised platform. Sometimes when a chilly night wind blew, we would put live coals under a table and sit around these coals, studying, reading or writing letters.

Eventually however, since the Indians had not attacked us, the owners of our house decided they wanted to live there themselves and we were offered a better built adobe block house. This house was near the jungle, but on the other side of town. Once again we were on the move.

While we were living there, one day soon after dinner; when most people were taking siestas, we heard children screaming near the house next to the jungle. Immediately we ran over and found that some Indians had come out of the jungle and had crept along a fence until they reached the patio where the children were playing. What the full intent of the Indians was we don't know but one of them threw a spear at a little boy which did no more than scratch the little fellow's chest. Almost as quickly as the Indians had come, armed Bolivian men on horseback also came in pursuit of the Indians. They never caught up to them because they were experts in hiding themselves in the jungle.

"Do you suppose they are going to ask us to move once again?" I asked Myron, after the excitement had passed, "I imagine that's just what will happen," he replied. "They are afraid the Indians will attack again, so the location is probably better for the missionaries."

We were right in our assumption. It wasn't long before the lady whose children were attacked by the Indians; and who owned the house next to the jungle, came one day and insisted that we trade houses with her. This lady had no real husband. She lived illegitimately with her sister's husband who was one of the prominent half German citizens of the community.

Two moves within eight months were enough so Myron arranged to buy the house; actually, there were two houses -- and about ten acres of ground, which included a large citrus fruit grove and banana patch. All of this for eight hundred dollars in United States currency.

We still had our two youngest children at home and although we lived next to the jungle for some time, we were never attacked. At a later date however, the Indians were once again discovered approaching the house we had vacated. There are probably two reasons why our former landlady and her children were objects of attack while we weren't. First, the Lord was caring for us. Psalm 91:2 "I will say of the Lord, He is my refuge and my fortress, my God;

in him will I trust." Secondly, the Indians considered our neighbors easy prey because there was only a mother and her children around the place most of the time and only occasionally a man was seen there at all.

Many years later, our oldest son Paul and his wife came to Bolivia to work with this same Indian tribe, but in a different location. During one visit with Paul and Marilyn, when Paul was introducing us to several who were then believers, one of the Indians, said, "Oh, we know who they are, we used to see them all the time when they lived at the village of Madrecitas. We were still unbelievers at that time and living in the jungle!" So the Indians had seen us much more often than we had seen them.

It is easy to look back now and see how the Lord protected us. There were times however, that our faith was really put to the test. For example, in moments of contemplation we could not help but ask ourselves the question, "Might not the savages slip out of the jungle and attack us as they had our neighbors?"

Then there were those occasions when Myron had to ride his horse alone through the jungle to visit people in other settlements or go the seven and one half miles to a ranch in Las Pocitas. This was our communication and supply link with the outside world. Myron tells of another occasion during a trip he made alone by night because the truck that traveled from the ranch to the city of Santa Cruz didn't arrive as scheduled. He felt just as secure and knew that the children and I were just as secure there as if we had been at home in the United States or Canada. The Lord has said to all who would serve Him, "Lo, I am with you always, even unto the end of the age." Matt. 28:20.

We were there in Madrecitas mainly to try and make contact with these Ayore Indians. There were also many opportunities for the sowing of the seed of God's Word to the Spanish speaking people of Madrecitas and the surrounding area. The sowing was not without opposition. As soon as the leaders of the established religion of Bolivia learned of our preaching and teaching in that area, they came to warn the people of our "heretical" beliefs and practices. As a result a few people who were previously friendly toward us turned cool, and temporarily there was lower attendance at our meetings. A couple of the young men would be present in our meetings, while the rest would raid the fruit trees. Sometimes we found pages missing from our hymn books.

However, there were also many times of encouragement when we had opportunity to share with different folks one on one. We can't say that many were saved, but the seed was sown. Our Heavenly Father is the Lord of the harvest. Luke 10:2.

It is generally agreed that the missionaries' first term on the field is usually the hardest because of the many adjustments one must make. We were no exception to the rule and for a very brief period of time at Madrecitas we were ready "to call it quits" and return to the United States. Oh how subtle is the enemy of the gospel. We went before the Lord and sought guidance through His Word.

Our own hearts told us that we could not be satisfied ministering the Word in any other place than right there in Madrecitas. I don't think it was the persecution that affected us as much as it was the general loneliness. There were long stretches of time without mail and without seeing another of our own people. Consequently it was with real joy that we received word that Jim and Ruth Dixon, who were newcomers to Bolivia, would soon join us in the work.

Myron immediately began readying the second house on our property for occupancy. This involved building an adobe wall in one room, adding doors and window shutters and re-roofing the entire house with new palm leaves. The roofing was delayed because the Bolivians believed that the palm should be cut only in a certain sign of the moon or it would rot. Incidentally, the Bolivian women washed clothes only in the "right sign" of the moon so that the clothes would not rot. We often wondered what it would be like if all the people in New York City lived according to that rule! Mahogany wood was plentiful, so these were the boards used for the doors. Often one board was as wide as a door, but each board had to be planed by hand. We even used mahogany for our pig trough.

After the Dixon family joined us, Jim and Myron would go on horseback regularly and leave gifts of knives, machettes or other inexpensive things along the trails for the Indians. Sometimes these were taken, but the men never saw any signs of life.

Of course it was always a very happy time when Paul and Ruth had their long vacations and could come home to be with us for awhile. They usually flew in our small mission plane to Las Pocitas. We would meet them there with an ox cart to take them those last seven and one half miles to Madrecitas. We decided that it was much safer and quicker to make that trip by ox cart rather than by truck, especially in the rainy season.

Then when it came time for the children to go back to school. I, along with Priscilla, would take them back to school, flying first to Santa Cruz where we could usually buy any item of clothing the children were needing for another school year.

On one occasion when David was celebrating his fourth birthday, he and Daddy were alone as Priscilla and I had made the trip out with Paul and Ruth. How thrilled David was when Daddy made a special birthday cake for him -- and that in the shape of a ship -- using two large sardine cans. They had a wonderful party all by themselves.

We were living in the days before radios were transistorized and could be operated by a few inexpensive batteries. We thought we had it made when we were able to purchase a radio powered by a rechargeable car battery. We hoped to keep this charged with a used wind charger which came from the United States as a gift to us.

We first bought a freshly charged battery from the city of Santa Cruz. We still sense the sheer ecstacy that came over us the first evening we used the radio and heard clearly in English the voice of Theodore Epp on the Back to the Bible broadcast. Then to top it off, that same evening, we heard them read a portion of a letter I had written to tell them how much one of their publications meant in the lives of our children! The blessing of hearing such broadcasts was short lived however, because the windcharger did not function properly and we had no other way to recharge the battery.

Communication by radio is a wonderful thing but there is another form of communication that is far more important. It is communication with God through prayer. We were a long time without rainfall. The water holes were drying up and the crops were failing. At one mid-week meeting it was reported to us that some people in a near-by district, who were opposed to the gospel, said that this was happening because we had been allowed to live in Madrecitas. This seemed to be a challenge. Could we believe God to answer prayer? In this meeting our hearts were challenged to believe God could and would do the impossible.

Myron told the people we would pray for rain. We did. We wanted them to see that we did believe that God could bring rain, and also that we were truly from God. We don't believe that it was mere coincidence that it rained yet that night and the next day, but it didn't rain nearly as much in the area where the people who had complained lived.

One evening there in Madrecitas, stands out in my memory. The meetings were usually held out in front of our house under a big tree. Some crude benches had been made so the people could sit down. When rainy season came, we tried to move some of the benches inside and have the service in what would have been called our living room. On this particular evening, I hadn't been feeling well, for we were expecting another child. Myron wondered if the meeting should be cancelled, because a heavy curtain was all that divided our living room from our bedroom and I was in bed. Just about the time Myron was beginning his message I knew that things weren't right and that I would probably suffer a miscarriage. How thankful I was that Ruth Dixon was there with us at the time.

Ruth and I were in the bedroom together, and she whispered, "What will we do?" "It will be O.K." I whispered in reply, "Just be sure the curtain is closed." I don't think anyone really knew what was going on in the bedroom just a curtain apart, for Myron was very surprised when he came in afterwards to see how I was doing.

Once again we found the Lord sufficient.

After a time, Myron experienced extreme physical weakness which even several days in bed did not correct. We sent a message by radio from the ranch in Las Pocitas, to our mission pilot Cliff Martz in Santa Cruz.

"Could Cliff come as soon as possible?" This was on a Friday afternoon and on Saturday we were overjoyed to hear and see a small yellow plane circling our house and then landing, not at the ranch, but in a pasture not far away. Cliff had chosen to risk this improvised airstrip in order to save Myron the tiring trip by horseback or ox cart to Las Pocitas. What a blessing Cliff was to us at that time.

Of course a crowd of people gathered around our plane. Many of them had never been close to an aircarft before. Goodbyes were said and Cliff and Myron were soon flying over the city of Santa Cruz. Upon landing there, Cliff sensed that something was wrong as soon as the tail of the plane touched the ground. An inspection revealed that the tail wheel assembly had struck a stump and had been damaged on take-off from the pasture. Thus, Cliff had literally risked his own safety in order to meet our need.

A check up by the doctor revealed that Myron's problems were mainly from malnutrition plus physical and nervous exhaustion.

We had been working in the extreme heat of the lowlands and the emotional strain of an imminent encounter with the savages had taken its toll too. All of us were considerably underweight. Myron weighed only one hundred and fifty-one pounds even though he was six foot four inches tall. Because of the high cost of canned foods we had to limit ourselves to three small cans of vegetables and two cans of fruit a week for our entire family. Rice was plentiful but fresh meat was hard to obtain even though we were in cattle country. We had tried hard to raise some vegetables, but the army ants would usually take care of any fresh sprouts overnight.

Doctors recommended a furlough. Myron was not able to return to Madrecitas, so I had the big job of breaking up our household and putting things in storage. We were so thankful that the Dixon family was there to carry on the work in our absence.

Once we were reunited as a family we went to our Mission headquarters in Cochabamba to await the Lord's provision for plane fares to the United States, and also to take care of other necessary papers we would need for travel.

Provisions were made and we were to begin our first furlough in the United States and Canada. Our days and weeks were filled with opportunities to fellowship with other Christians and to make the needs of Bolivia known throughout Michigan and other areas of the United States. The love of friends and family meant so much.

Furlough Begins

Chapter 6

Getting ready for furlough is always a busy time. It requires packing away things that are going to stay, packing the few things that will go home with us, and at the same time trying to keep an eye on the children.

It was just the day before we were to travel. The children were playing with others on the back porch of the Mission home, and found it a lot of fun to jump up on and off those barrels of packed household items. Priscilla was just four years old and always wanted to try and keep up with her big brothers and sister. Unfortunately, when she made an attempt to jump off the barrel, she jumped a little too far and landed a few feet below the porch on the ground, and that face first. We were so thankful that nothing was broken, but she did have a badly bruised face, which seemed to get blacker with assorted colors as each day passed. She was the one the grandparents and relatives hadn't seen.

We went directly to Canada with a couple of hours layover in Montreal before we flew on to Ottawa. My two aunts who had been supporting us regularly were at the airport to meet us. We had planned to spend the two hours together visiting. Apparently when they got the first glimpse of that skinny undernourished family they were filled with alarm. But when they saw our little four year old---oh my! "You all looked just sick! I hid behind a pole so you wouldn't see my tears, I just couldn't understand what had happened to Priscilla." Yes, her face was quite a bit blacker with each day of our travels. Even the stewardess had taken pity on her as well as the other children and brought them all sorts of treats.

Chapter 6

We were to stay the first three months in Joy's folk's summer home. It was a real provision of the Lord, giving a wonderful time of rest which we needed so badly. On one occasion soon after we arrived, my mother said, "Well, I trust you aren't thinking of returning, there is surely a lot of missionary work here to do as well as there!" Yes, we knew there were people to be reached with the gospel in our homeland too, but what about the many Christians who lived here? How wonderful it would be if every Christian sought to witness for Christ and to lead that one to know him as Saviour. Our hearts were in Bolivia because we had seen the need of untouched people. We knew the Lord would lead when it came to the time of our return.

Furlough for a missionary is an experience in faith just as much as his time on the field. Sometimes we abounded in material things and at other times, like the Apostle Paul, we were abased. But, at about the time our last dollar was spent, we could expect the Lord to do something unusual for us.

I remember especially the trip we made from Michigan to our training center in California during the late spring and summer of 1954. We traveled in our station wagon; it was loaded in such a way that two of our children could stretch out on top of the baggage in the back while the two smaller ones could nap fairly comfortably on the back seat. While making a stop at a friend's home in Missouri, we received an unexpected medical bill for one hundred and seventy dollars. This took a great deal of our cash but we continued westward anyway. In Nebraska we had a meeting and friends gave us ten dollars and twenty cents, but at the same time in Nebraska we had a blowout which necessitated our buying a new tire and tube for twenty-five dollars. After this we knew there would be no more motels, so drove straight through to California. In times of unbelief we would ask the Lord, "What will we do if we run out of money or break down?" The Lord seemed to say to us, "Believe me!" He remained faithful and we didn't break down or run completely out of money. We arrived at Boot Camp with two dollars and fifty cents in our pockets!

It was always customary we knew from experience that one should stop and get groceries in town before coming into camp. Still we were to believe the Lord!

When we arrived in camp they were just beginning a missionary conference. Not as many outsiders came as they expected, so we were asked to take meals all that week in the dining hall -- free of charge. God is faithful!

It was good to be in boot camp once again with students whose objective was to reach the unreached people of the world with the Gospel of Jesus Christ. There was an opportunity to serve too. We taught Spanish to those who thought the Lord was directing them toward South America.

This was also a time of looking to the Lord for some equipment. We felt we needed certain things to take back with us, as well as passage back to Bolivia. Some of our friends and supporters thought we should not return to Bolivia for reasons of health, but eventually they changed their minds as they saw the abundant way the Lord supplied for our return. One of the outstanding provisions was a Jeep station wagon. This was sold to us at a very reasonable price by a young woman whose husband was burned to death in a forest fire in California. Several of our men had volunteered their assistance in fighting the fire.

Along with the blessings there were what seemed to be hindrances from the enemy. Paul broke his arm while trying to ride a motor bike. Also, while I was washing out some packing barrels with excessively hot water in the camp laundry room, the hose broke, spraying almost boiling water on both my legs. I suffered third degree burns on one leg, and still had some bandages on that leg when we arrived back in Bolivia.

It was suggested that we might return to Bolivia more cheaply with our equipment if we were to go by ship rather than plane.

First came proving the Lord's faithfulness once again as we traveled back across the States. There were meetings and final good-byes to relative and friends. We flew from Miami to Nassau in the Bahamas where we were to board an English ship, La Reina Del Pacifico. Our ship was a day late so we had a day and night to spend there in Nassau. We were traveling fourth class, but this didn't seem to bother any of us. We experienced quite a bit of seasickness, but there were days when the Lord just gave us a relaxing time of rest. The children always seemed to find things to do while playing on deck.

We arrived at Arica, Chile, our port of disembarkation, two weeks after our departure from Nassau. Since Arica had just been made a "free port", all hotels were filled. There were missionaries in the city, of course, who graciously gave us lodging until we could take a train to Bolivia. We learned that it never rains in Arica, so all fresh water is brought in from other areas. It proved to be an unforgettable experience. Our trip was made by narrow gauge railroad from Arica, Chile to La Paz, Bolivia. Had we been able to make reservations well in advance, we could have enjoyed the comfort of berths and private compartments at a very nominal fee. As it was we had to stand in line at the station in Arica for over an hour to purchase tickets of any kind. Once the gates were open, the mob of people rushing to get seats on the train was much like a herd of animals stampeding. David and Priscilla, our two youngest, were nearly trampled and began to cry.

We were able to secure two empty seats -- more literally wood benches, each one just wide enough to take three of us.

Our train finally departed at 9:20 p.m. It jerked and seemed to have great difficulty ascending the steep grades in the mountains. At times it appeared that the engineer would back down a grade and try again but it was so dark we really couldn't tell. At the Bolivian border, we were required to change trains and would have made a run for some seats; but we were too sick from the high altitude and the motion of the train.

The train was packed with Aymara Indians who were probably engaged in contraband trade. They carried everything from fresh meat to whiskey and wine. Some drank freely of the latter which contributed to the mess in which we found ourselves. The restrooms were filled with live chickens and other cargo so if one had an upset stomach, as many did, he stuck his head out of the window. If he had to relieve himself in some other way, he had to dash outside when the train made a stop. That is why train and bus stops in Bolivia are some of the filthiest places imaginable. It's not that some restaurant and hotel owners don't try to provide facilities; it's that many of the indigenous people don't know how to use them and therefore any semblance of a restroom becomes unusable in a very short time.

At about midnight we were in the first village before La Paz when the train broke down. Since we were told there would be a delay of about two hours, a lady from New York, who was also a passenger on the train, and Myron telephoned for a "taxi" to come for us from La Paz. We were required to pay in advance. We should have known better because the taxi never came. Eventually the train got underway and we arrived at the "alta" of La Paz which is the high plateau of thirteen thousand five hundred feet, where we disembarked and hired another taxi to take us to the city which was one thousand feet lower. During our trip from Arica, we probably traveled to heights of seventeen thousand feet on the train.

Whether our missionary hosts were happy to be awakened at that early hour. I'm not sure, but they were gracious and we were thankful to be in a clean room, get a drink of pure water and go to bed.

We had suffered a small amount of discomfort for a short while; how much more have Christians before us suffered that we might have the Word of God today.

New Beginings

Chapter 7

Before we came home on furlough it was mutually agreed by our field leaders and us that if we were to have reasonably good health we would have to work in an area where the climate was moderate and where nourishing food was available. This would rule out our return to Madrecitas. Where should we work? We looked to the Lord for the answer and it was waiting us at our Mission headquarters in Cochabamba.

For years the Bolivian health department had operated a leprosarium not too far from Tambo, our school for missionary children. But this leprosarium had become a disgrace to the Bolivian government. At least two of the so-called doctors in charge had been dishonest to the point that food, drugs and clothing designated for the lepers were sold to the public. There were other injustices also with the consequence that many of the patients escaped rather than suffer hunger and mistreatment at the leprosarium.

Government officials didn't just implore us as a mission to take over the work, they practically insisted. It was not a practice of New Tribes Mission to have institutional ministries on our fields, which would take away the ministry to the tribal work. However, the home chairman of our Mission, who was in Bolivia at the time of our return from furlough, and our field chairman asked us if we would head up the work at the leprosarium. Myron would have the general oversight of the work and I, under the supervision of Dr. John White who was then with our mission in Bolivia, would carry on the nursing ministry. Our responsibility would begin as soon as the Bolivian officials could discharge the present director from his post.

Knowing that things usually move slowly in Bolivia, we considered what we should do in the meantime. Near the leprosarium were a couple of villages without a consistent gospel witness. Both were visited occasionally on Sundays by some of our Tambo staff and older students, not without opposition from the local religious leaders. In the one called Pampagrande, the persecution reached the point of stoning. We considered settling there temporarily but no one would rent us a house. We settled in the other village called Mataral. There was already at least one Christian and living quarters were made available to us.

Before we could make this move however, it was necessary for Myron to make a trip back to Madrecitas in order to sell the house and bring out our belongings which had been stored there. The Dixon family had moved from there to the Santa Cruz mission home. What was going to happen to the work there? We learned that this same group of Indians had come out of the jungle in a friendly manner to camps where missionaries were working with others of the same tribe. Our well established work is still there in what is called Tobite. Our own Paul and Marilyn worked with this same group for many years. Although now living and working elsewhere they still have a vital part in the ministry.

From the time we moved to Mataral, we knew the Lord's blessing in the work. We held meetings in what was our living room. Many trips were made by horseback out into the surrounding countryside and there was a hunger for the gospel. People wanted to listen. As mentioned, there was at least one believer whom we met. As the word was taught many others believed and came to know the Lord Jesus as their own personal Saviour. Among these were two men, Juan and Ricardo, who were political enemies. Juan accused Ricardo of having shot his brother several years earlier in a political battle. Both attended our services but would not speak to each other and sat on opposite sides of the room. One evening just before Myron was to close the service, Juan rose to his feet and said, "Don Mario (Mr. Myron), the whole world knows that things aren't right between Don Ricardo and me. I don't want our prayers hindered here; I want him to forgive me!" They embraced one another and continued close friends and witnessed together for the Lord until Ricardo's death several years later. What a testimony this was to the town's people who took note of the difference Christ had made in the lives of these two men. Others came to know the Lord. There was a large Sunday School established and weekly we saw new faces in the group. We were only in Mataral ten months, but there is a small but flourishing church there now with Don Juan still standing true as its leader.

A couple of experiences worth relating are associated with the largest "hotel" in the village. I must explain that a hotel in Bolivia may be an eating place with a bed or two for guests and may range from a palm roofed hut to a structure comparable to our hotels in the United States. The hotel I write about was a rather pretentious sprawling structure of adobe and cement situated at the main intersection of our village. It contained a dining hall and several guest rooms.

The maids employed there were poorer girls and women who were glad for sleeping quarters, food and a pittance of a wage in exchange for their services. One such woman (there didn't seem to be any husband) had a sick baby which she brought for me to see. It was only skin and bones. The reason; the mother had lost her ability to nurse the child and could not afford to buy any kind of milk with which to feed the baby. You see, good dairy cows are not plentiful in Bolivia and only the wealthier people can afford to purchase imported powdered or condensed milk. It was obvious to us that the baby was really starving to death so we agreed to care for him in our home until he was again healthy. It would have been so easy for us, many times, to have started an orphanage in Bolivia because wherever we went we found so many children who lacked the essentials of life. Within a matter of weeks this baby had gained weight and was well. We returned him to his mother with suggestions as to what simple foods she could prepare for him. However, it seemed that the owners of the hotel wouldn't provide even these simply foods and so the child died.

Our other connection with this hotel and it's owners, a man and his wife, came in the purchase of a three roomed house from them, for our own living quarters and a meeting room. One of the new believers, who was supposed to be knowledgeable about legal transactions, assisted Myron in drawing up a purchase contract. We were to make a down payment with the final payment at a later date. The man signed and Myron signed. Everything seemed in order and we went about fixing up the house as most Americans do. Several months later when Myron was about to make the final payment, we received a message from the local magistrate saying that the purchase could not be consummated because the wife of the owner had never agreed to the sale. The truth was that both the husband and the wife recognized that the house was now worth much more than when we had moved into it and they wished to reap the benefits by merely refunding the down payment. Well, the local judge told us that they had legal grounds for their actions and advised us to settle out of court as best we could. We lost money through trickery, but it worked out better from a spiritual standpoint. Had we retained the house, we likely would have left it for the believers to use as a meeting place. But since it was taken from us, we had nothing to leave. So they were required to build a place with their own resources. That was much better, spiritually speaking for them.

There is a sequel to the story however which confirms the cliche, "crime does not pay." We are told that the owner of the hotel took the profit he made on the house and went to Brazil where he purchased considerable contraband merchandise. But, not being an expert in such ilicit business, he lost everything when his merchandise was confiscated by custom agents. We were also told that his wife's comment was, "And all because of the foreigners!"

And then it happened! Of all the inconvenient times for Myron, my hubby, to be sick! And in the hospital having an appendectomy! We had known for months that the Bolivian government wanted us to take over the leper colony between Cochabamba and Santa Cruz -- just a few kilometers from Mataral, and now the call had come! Would someone from our Mission please meet the Minister of Health down at the Colony, and receive the charge formally from his hands? And "in secret please. The public must not know until the transaction is formalized."

What did I know about leprosy? The Minister of Health insisted that this was not an immediate concern. They had plenty of information to pass on to us. But for now the Colony needed caring hearts, people that were honest to give out the stated medication for each, and that would feed and clothe the sick ones as the government sent in the funds. Government men had studied our mission incognito, and felt sure we would not exploit the lepers by using their clothing, food and funds for our own profit....as others had.

Two people volunteered to represent Myron down at the colony--Stan Johnson, our field director, and Jean Dye who would stay on for a week until Myron and I could take over. They picked me up at Mataral. As soon as the Minister of Health met us, they asked us to wait while he surprised the paramedic then in charge of the Colony, who was to lose his job. He made sure the paramedic terminated any connection with that house, and came with us to round up the lepers for a meeting.

I still remember that get-together! The minister of health allowed the paramedic to speak first: "You're going to have others looking after you now," he said, "And you'll probably have it better because these Americans have money...."

That was about it. My heart sank. Of all the things we could never be known for it was money! If only the truth were known about how we had lived during our first four-year term in Bolivia! No fixed salary. Completely "by faith" in God alone. And this term so far was no different. Nor were we to be paid by the government!

The the Minister of Health took over. He himself had run into New Tribers on occasion in the interior of Bolivia. And he himself cared about the state of the lepers.

"These missionaries will be in charge of you now," he said. "And I do not say they have money. But they have something else. They have love," he emphasized.

As soon as he said that, I noticed that some of the women standing in the group burst into tears. Then he explained that Myron, the new administrator, would be joining them in a week or so, and that I, the nurse, would move in within a week.

Jean Dye would "hold down" the administrator's house up the hill and come down for a visit each morning. She had brought along some translation work and was not expected to start anything before we arrived.

How we did appreciate Jean's willingness to help out in this way. The house was far from comfortable or clean; nevertheless, undaunted, Jean stayed there until I was able to move our belongings from Mataral.

The thirty one patients interned at the colony when it was turned over to us were in a most deplorable state. Most lived in little mud shacks with leaky roofs and -- if fortunate -- had one ragged blanket for warmth. They lacked both food and clothing. There was no hospital and no medicines. We were told that what items had been appropriated by the Bolivian government were sold to the public by the former director of the colony.

The children and I moved into our unfinished house near the "highway". How thankful we were for Cliff and Virginia Martz who were at that time in Tambo and came to help us move. Everyone was so kind. This four room adobe house which had been used as a food storeroom, we were to call home. It was very much unfinished with it's rough mud walls, dirt floors and only holes for windows. The place was overrun with rats.

In addition to the rather trying situation, Priscilla, almost five years old, fell into the river which flowed near the house and would have drowned had not her brother Paul pulled her out. Another incident in those beginning days was when Paul swallowed some kerosene while he was siphoning it from a barrel for use in our kitchen stove. He became very ill and was in bed for over a week.

Needless to say, it was a happy day when Myron arrived from Cochabmba.

There was so much to be done everywhere, but this did not hinder us from beginning Bible studies with the people immediately; in addition to seeing that they had food and medical care. Although the Bible study times were voluntary, almost everyone attended as we met under one of the big trees. All seemed to be interested in the Word of God. We began to see those who came to us telling us that they wanted to be saved.

What a time of rejoicing! With the teaching of the Word, we saw these new babes in Christ begin to grow spiritually and we noticed a great difference in their attitudes towards others in the camp.

However, not all received the Lord. The story had been related to us several times about an incident that happened before we came to the colony. One man had helped hang another patient in retaliation for this man's reporting to authorities the theft of cattle. It seems that some of the patients and a former director of the colony had killed cattle that grazed on colony land, and had sold the meat in a distant city. The director was dismissed from office but never punished in any other way. The other wrong doers continued as patients in the colony. They were our trouble makers. Certain patients were always quick to point out to us a tree that slanted over the colony road from which the victim was hung. They also told us that this man believed just as we missionaries taught. Could he have been a believer? It is quite possible.

Most patients needed blankets and clothing. Missionaries gave of that which they had. Patients well enough to work needed work, so we paid the men for clearing roads, repairing roofs and cutting weeds which were waist high everywhere. Women were paid for washing clothes and bed linen for others too sick to care for themselves.

Treatment time came daily, when I would check the patients for perforating ulcers, change bandages, and give out their daily medication. Some suffered severe reactions. In those first days daily IV's had to be administered to all. It was a happy day when this same medication came in pill form. Or was it? This created more problems because the Bolivian people have the supposition that pills are not as good as injections. Often we would find those same pills on the ground. The patients had just thrown them away. It became necessary for each one to take his dosage in my presence.

New patients were arriving daily, not only one or two at a time, but sometimes by the truckload. Oh how our hearts cried out to the Lord to continue to give strength for each day. We wanted to meet the needs of these dear people who were disowned, unloved, and uncared for. This was the time we usually saw those who had received the Lord show that they belonged to Him.

"Don Mario," which is what they called Myron, "we can move over and give a place for one or two to sleep in our little house." This was such an encouragement to both of us. Nevertheless, our hearts sank every time new patients arrived. Where would we put them? This was always a big question in our minds.

I was "on call" day and night. It wasn't unusual for one of the patients to come in the middle of the night. After a loud clapping of their hands to awaken us or to get our attention, I would hear, "Senora, senora, please come quickly, Alejandro is very sick!" or "Margarita is about to have her baby, can you come quickly?"

In the meantime, workmen were finishing our house. Lath for the ceiling was made of split cactus wood which is quite strong and durable if dried properly. The plastering was then done in three stages. First a coating of mud and grass was applied. The next coating would be a layer of mud and manure and finally an application of lime. Each application required several days to dry. Can you imagine what we encountered in dust, dirt and odor each day when we returned home from our work with the patients? Each evening was spent cleaning up the mess and although we daily became physically and emotionally exhausted, we experienced a deep satisfaction because we knew we were in God's place for us and doing His will.

Incidentally, our four room house also became a temporary home to Dr. White and his family. Fortunately, by the time they arrived we had added a lean-to store room at the back of our house where our boys slept when they were home from school.

Upon examining the patients more thoroughly, Dr. White found that several of them should have appendectomies. But, where could he operate where there was no dust or the chance of mud falling from a tile roof? The answer: our dining room! Our dining room table became the operating table.

Many were the times during our doctor's visit to the colony, I heard, "Joy, could you prepare the patient for surgery?" All pre-operative preparations were done in their little mud huts. After this they were brought to our house in our Jeep where the operations were performed. Then the patient was returned to their own homes before they were even awake again. Sometimes they could hardly believe that they had been in our home.

Sometimes an appendix or other organ which the doctor wished to examine microscopically later would end up in our refrigerator. One particular day after surgery, Lorrie White was getting our lunch. The doctor and I had returned to the colony with the patient and Myron and Lorrie were there at home. "What is this Myron? Is it still edible?" "Oh my, no!" was Myron's response. "That container should have been clearly marked, 'For Dr. John'." It could have ended up in our spaghetti dish for lunch! A sense of humor was our tonic many times. Aren't we glad that the Lord gave us that sense of humor?

The Lord also provided more staff to help in the work of the Leper Colony because new patients continued to arrive. Ed and Neva Miller came with their son Roddy. Ed had been helping out in the building of the school for missionary children before coming to work with us at the Colony.

Paul and Beulah Mason had joined our staff as missionary dentists. What a blessing they were. Until their coming, the people could do nothing but suffer from toothache because no professional dentist in Bolivia would have touched a leper. At first, Dr. White suggested that all of us who were in direct contact with the patients take small amounts of the drug to be used as a preventative. Later however, he concluded that in doing this we might build up an immunity to the drug and therefore be without medical help if we did contract the disease. So, we did nothing but use caution, and trusted the Lord to protect all who were there. A couple of single ladies, Gwen Chapman and Eleanor Lahue were also helping for several months, working with the children as well as helpers with the patients in the hospital. Les and Evelyn Thompson, two former teachers in our mission school, came to work with us. Les was our handyman; while Evelyn helped with the record keeping of all of our patients. Later Carl and Ruth Ziegler also joined our staff.

We had many children in the colony who had been exposed to the disease because of their parents. We realized more and more how much a school for the children was going to be needed. Yarmela Jelinek came to live in the colony as their teacher. Marge Day, who worked with the Yura Indians, was our lab technician. She would pay a visit to the colony every six months in order to help me with the skin analysis. Many hours would be spent over her little microscope -- which she brought with her. Analysis results were important to all patients. It would tell us whether the disease was arrested. A clear negative diagnosis had to be obtained three times in succession before a patient could be discharged. How discouraging it was to receive one or two negatives, then receive a positive in the next analysis. Marge Day was also a tremendous help to us during the necessary surgeries, which we always tried to postpone until she was with us.

Good News Arrives

Chapter 8

What good news our mail brought to us one day! We hadn't had mail in a long time and were hungry for word from home, loved ones, and friends. Upon opening one of our letters what joy came to our hearts. It was from a couple in California.

We wrote at a former time about the surgery we had to perform in our makeshift hospital. The only protection from falling dust and dirt, being the sheet Marge Day and I managed to hang above our makeshift operating table. We were just telling things 'as they were' to the folk back home. This particular couple, Dick and Lois Kingham were challenged to come to the field of Bolivia on a temporary basis to help build a new hospital. How thrilled we were! Our excitement knew no end. Several months later Dick and Lois with their two children arrived on the field.

It was a day of much rejoicing when the hospital was started. We "prayed in" materials and the Lord provided them. No, this building didn't compare, of course, to a hospital in the United States and Canada, but it was clean and adequate. It was built of adobe locks, with a tile roof. Inside walls and ceilings were plastered. The floors were cement. There were actually glass windows and solid doors. Such a difference from the one in which we had been working.

The two Kingham children were enrolled in our Mission boarding school, just an hour's drive from the colony. The whole family fitted in so well. They were with us a little over two years until the hospital was finished.

While Dick Kingham was building the hospital, working many hours a day, he developed a pain in his shoulder. He didn't pay any attention to it, saying, "Oh, it's just from all the hammering I've been doing!" Approximately one year after they returned home, the Lord called Dick Home to be with Himself. He suffered a severe case of rapid moving multiple sclerosis.

What did we do for beds for the hospital? Up to the time the hospital was finished, all bed patients -- those who suffered reactions to the medication -- had to remain in their homes. Now they could be housed in the hospital, making it easier to care for them. Beds were made by using palm branch slats.

One of our dear ladies in the mission school, "Mom" Janofski had come to Bolivia to serve at the age of 65. Her family was grown, and her daughter, Mabel Hurst, was also a missionary in Bolivia. Mom came to the school for missionary children to be of help where needed. That included mending, running an after-school snack shop for the children, and agreeing to do almost anything that was handed to her. She was truly "Mom" to all. It was Mom who sewed many sacks or bags which in turn were filled with straw for mattresses and pillows for our hospital beds. She also made lovely quilts -- pieces taken from discarded children's clothing -- for each bed in the hospital. Yes, everything was very simple, but in contrast to what the patients had in their homes it was almost luxurious.

Mom Janofski was still in Bolivia when the Lord took her HOME. She is buried in our little cemetery next to a small air strip at the school.

Many of our co-laborers there shared what they had to furnish the hospital with sheets, pillow cases, etc. When a patient was hospitalized, he came with a small basket containing his tin plate, spoon and cup. For a very small wage, we were able to hire one of the patients to cook for those in the hospital.

Many of our other needs were met by Christians back home. Ladies made bandages from old sheets. We were so happy that these came through at least for a time, custom free. They were invaluable to us. Some made hospital gowns for use in the hospital. Others collected boxes of used clothing for all of our patients. Even toys were sent to the children.

Our numbers constantly grew and before many months passed we had over 100 patients to care for.

A NEW PATIENT ARRIVES

Our family was having our evening meal. It was school vacation time. We relished those times together. The children had finished eating and Daddy said they could go outside for a while so that we could "sit a minute" over our coffee before we had our family devotions together. It was so peaceful and quiet! Not for long however, for we heard Paul call out, "Daddy, Mommy, a lady just got off the back of a truck which stopped in front of our house. She is coming, but she is crying!"

Elda had arrived! She had grown up in the city of La Paz, the daughter of a well-to-do merchant. She was dressed better than most of our patients and from outward appearance didn't seem too disfigured by the disease. We invited her to sit a moment on our front porch while we talked with her. Yes, she had been to many doctors in La Paz and couldn't seem to get any help. Then her family told her there was no more money for doctor bills. When the doctors were informed of this, they said, "Well, you have leprosy and you will have to go to the Colony in Los Negros to be treated."

"They took all of our money, then gave me this bad news," Elda said, "I couldn't even get anyone to let me ride in the bus or in a cab of a truck. They treated me like dirt,"

Elda was very bitter. For some time she wouldn't attend our morning devotions in the colony or the Bible studies. She would say, "If there was a God, he wouldn't let me get in this condition." Oh how we prayed for Elda, and others were praying too for we had mentioned her name in our letters.

It didn't help much either when Dr. John in his examination said that it would be best to amputate the toes of one foot because of infection and deterioration.

I spent much time with Elda, praying at the same time as I was dressing her wounds that the Lord would give me just the right things to say. Little by little she began to listen. She began to attend our Bible studies -- sitting at the back of the group. We knew she was there and that she was listening. What a tremendous thrill it was one day, after I had been talking with her for some time that she said, "Oh, Senora, I want to accept Jesus as my Savior!" Tears filled my eyes and I could hardly speak out but said, "Let's pray together, Elda. You tell the Lord why you need Him in your life and ask Him to come in." She prayed, "Lord Jesus, you know my heart is bad and sinful and disfigured just like my body is disfigured by this awful disease of leprosy. Please come into my heart. Take away my bitterness and make me clean." That was the beginning of a changed heart and life. She later became a very valuable worker and helper to me in the hospital.

There were many others who came to know the Lord as their Saviour.

Constance, for example, was a blind lady. As a result of the disease she had lost the sight in both eyes. She was our first believer. We thrilled at her testimony. She, along with many others, was baptized in the little river which flowed through the colony. She and her husband -- who was among the first believers -- became a testimony to others of God's saving Grace.

Chapter 8

In Matthew 7:16 and 20, we read "Ye shall know them by their fruits." How true this is. Even though many did come to know the Lord as their Savior, there were others whose sincerity we doubted. It seemed their so called conversions were only for the purpose of gaining favor with the staff. Lust and greediness showed up in many ways.

There was always a constant flow of visitors to the colony from all over Bolivia. We delighted in their visits, for we knew when they left they would be praying for us. We counted on the prayers of God's people. Los Negros, or the leper colony, was on the one main road between Cochabamba in the highlands and Santa Cruz in the lowlands. Because of this, many of our co-workers traveling this road would stop for a visit. They were all welcome.

AND THEN THERE WERE WEDDINGS

As we stated earlier in the book, we discouraged as much as possible couples living together illegitimately. However, we also had to consider the culture of the people in Bolivia. Many folk can't afford to pay for even a civil ceremony, and because of this are just living together. When the Word of God was taught over a period of time in the Colony, we had some couples feel they weren't pleasing God by living together. We would arrange for the official from the neighboring town to come to our house. Many "weddings" were held on our back porch.

However, we did have another very interesting wedding there in the Colony too. One of our single lady workers, Gwen Chapman and Ben Estil were married. Ben had been a visitor to the colony on several occasions, and although they had considered the matter of marriage for some time none of us really knew about it until a week before it happened. It meant a lot of hurrying around but the civil marriage was performed on Sunday morning in Pampa Grande and the wedding ceremony in the colony on Sunday afternoon. Myron married them, I was matron of honor and Mel Wyma best man. It was a real blessing to every one who attended. Following the ceremony, cake and pop were served to everyone at the colony and later at our house Neva Miller and I had a lunch prepared. There were at least twenty five from the school that had come by truck. However, they arrived at five o'clock instead of three thirty when the wedding was scheduled. The delay was caused by motor trouble. Nevertheless the school chorus sang in the colony and also at Mataral in the evening. The newlyweds left the next day. Yes, we still found time to visit those believers in Mataral on a regular basis, usually once a week. They needed the continuous teaching of the Word, as well as the new converts in the colony.

Chapter 8

"A DAY OFF"

On one of the visits of Dr. John and his family to the colony he talked with Myron and me about taking more time off. It just seemed impossible to even think of it, especially to be gone for a full day. However, after praying about the matter the Lord seemed to lead and we decided to take our day off by driving to our mission school to be with the family. Unknown to us, Dr. White had also suggested to the staff at the school that I might be available to give some piano lessons -- on my day off. So after taking an early morning trip to the hospital to check on things there, and leaving instructions for my helpers, we took off for the school. Teaching began about ten o'clock and continued until lunch time, then from one until five in the afternoon.

After supper we headed back to the colony, made our nightly checkup on things in the hospital, and finally got into bed about midnight. Sometimes we didn't think it was worth the effort, but it was a change and we were thankful to be able to help in this way at the mission school.

In spite of our day off, we ourselves continued to have more health problems. The grips of malaria seem to come to first one of us then the other. Many days were discouraging and we would begin to ask ourselves, "Are the folk back home praying? Surely we are not in this warfare alone." Yes, we were faint and discouraged, but God was faithful to encourage through His Word. We discovered as we spent time in the Word, that the threefold source of God's peace was first to trust, then submit to what God had for us, and then to obey His commands. No, we were not in the battle alone; God was with us every moment of each day and night too. How encouraging the verse in Isaiah 43:2 was to each of us. "When thou passest through the water, I will be with thee; and through the rivers, they shall not overflow thee; when thou walkst through the fire, thou shalt not be burned, neither shall the flame kindle upon thee." Over and over again we read God's command to "fear not!" God knew just what we were experiencing.

As time went on, the promises the Bolivian government had made to us were forgotten. The agreement to give a certain amount each month in money and medications was not kept. Perhaps they felt that because they had so-called "rich Americans" handling the work they didn't need to keep their side of the agreement. However, new patients continued to arrive. Although faint at heart, we knew we must continue to go on.

Myron made several trips to La Paz to talk with the officials. Each time it seemed that things would be better; then their help would slack off once again. On one of Myron's trips to La Paz, the children were all home for vacation from school. It was good to have them there, especially when I came down with another attack of malaria. One incident stands out clearly in my mind. I was in bed with quite a high fever. I kept on feeling a tickling at the back of my neck, and I shrugged it off thinking it was just the fever causing the sensation. What a surprise I received when I reached back at one point and realized that I had a snake in bed with me. I might have felt weak, but I took that reptile and slung it across the room as hard as I could then called, "Paul, please come quick!" For a while he found it difficult to find the snake again, but was able to locate it behind our makeshift closet and showed his 'bravery' in bringing it to it's death. I don't' really know if that snake was poisonous or not, but once again the Lord's hand was upon us in protecting from all harm. Our house wasn't built tight like houses are in the United States and Canada.

One time when Myron was away he brought back a gift for me in the form of two canaries. My how we all enjoyed those birds. They each had a beautiful song, and would sing all day long, and especially so when we would come back home from work. They were indeed a part of the family. I always covered the cage at night, for the house was drafty, and cool in the evenings and nights. One morning I got up, uncovered the cage as usual and was surprised to find both canaries gone! The cage seemed to be intact, and the door closed, and all we could find were a couple feathers in the bottom of the cage. It was a mystery. Where did those birds go? They were nowhere to be found in the living room where their cage had been or in the kitchen. When we searched the bedrooms, we suddenly found the culprit. There curled around the wood supports of that makeshift closet in our bedroom was a very large snake. And it was a poisonous one. What could we do? Just about that time, four of the patients came to the house. We told them our problem. "Oh, we know how to get him out! "As a rule, the patients did not come into our home, but we visited on the porch outside. In this case, however, we didn't care whether they were patients or not. We let them take care of the problem and they did by each bringing into the bedroom a large forked branch. With these implements two of the men pinned the snake down, while the other two killed it. Then they carried it outside. Upon inspection, we noticed that the snake had two small humps in it. Yes, there's where we found our canaries!

At the end of five years, we wondered if we should not begin making plans for another furlough. Our field chairman thought so too. It had been a strenuous five years since our last one and it seemed best that we have a rest and change before we became too run down in health and strength as we were at the end of our first term in Bolivia. Then too, our Jeep station wagon was constantly breaking down with one problem or another and we hoped that we might be able to bring back a new vehicle from the States.

Incidentally, what is a furlough and why should a missionary return to his homeland once very five years or so? We should say, first of all, that a furlough is not a year of complete rest and inactivity so a missionary can regain his strength. A furlough is really a leave of absence from one's duties during which time he can: re-evaluate his work from a distance, then also report to supporting churches and friends through messages and pictures. These folk had been faithful to us in prayer and giving and they indeed had a right to hear what has been accomplished by the Lord working through us as His vessels. It is also a time to recruit others for the task of world evangelism. How many times our co-workers worked alone. The field is "white unto harvest," but "laborer are few." Mixed in with these is the joy of reunion with loved ones and friends and a reacquaintance with MacDonald's Golden Arches and some other pleasures not found on the field of service.

Our actual furlough began the following June, after some tearful farewells by both the staff and patients at the leprosarium and the believers outside the colony in the church in Mataral and from our Bible study groups. We had seen fifty people give testimony of their faith through baptism (forty-three from the colony and seven from Mataral) during our five and one half year term of service. Truly the Lord was good!

Of course one can't just walk away from his work on the field without someone there to take up the ministry. The Lord provided a couple of RN's from England, Hudson and Joan Birkett, to come and fill the gap while we were on furlough. They were able to arrive a couple of months before we left and so our hearts were at ease, knowing the colony was being cared for. Paul Mason took on the responsibility of overseeing the work as a whole while Myron and I were away.

Our itinerary by plane from Cochabamba included stops at La Paz, Bolivia and Lima, Peru, where we spent the weekend at the airline's expense. Here the children were impressed by the many neon lights. It was here also we saw what are supposed to be Pizzaro's bones encased in a glass coffin. It was here too, that a pickpocket relieved Myron of his billfold. He must have been disappointed though, because the billfold was twelve years old and contained nothing but a couple of identification papers for Bolivia. Myron had purposely carried his money in another pocket. Further landings were made in both Quayaquil and Quito, Ecuador before arriving in Miami, Florida. How hot it was in Florida compared to the cool mountains of Bolivia!

Upon purchasing a used car in Florida, we started our travel northward, ministering in mission training centers, churches and Bible camps along the way. We made stops in Missouri, Tennessee, Kentucky, West Virginia, Ontario, Quebec, again to Ontario and finally two months later to Clarksville, Michigan where once again Christian friends from the Clarksville Bible Church provided us with a home for a year.

Being in a home of our own didn't mean we were to discontinue our travels. Almost every weekend found us going somewhere in Michigan as a family for meetings. During the months of February and March, Myron traveled in meetings by himself as the four children were in school. There were stops in Illinois, Missouri, Colorado, New Mexico, Arizona, California, Nevada and back again to Michigan. By the time he arrived home in Clarksville the little two-door Ford was so packed with rolled bandages and other contributions for the colony that they literally rolled out as he opened the car door.

About this time the Lord provided us with a new Chevrolet carryall to take back to Bolivia. Myron began once more to build packing boxes, and I seemed to immediately fill them with things for the field. When after a fond farewell we left Clarksville late in May, we left behind us the Chevy carryall and twenty five pieces of cargo which, with considerable difficulty, the Bible Church shipped to us later. What a furlough! In retrospect, it seemed like a whirlwind, but how faithful the Lord had been through His people to supply our every need and see us back in Bolivia exactly one year from the time of our departure.

Home In Los Negros

Chapter 9

Upon arriving in Cochabamba at the close of our second furlough, we wondered how we would fare with the Bolivian custom officials. We had a considerable amount of baggage. We had been praying and we knew many others were praying too. The result: no customs officials were on hand so we were told to walk on through the gates!

Being in Cochabamba meant that we were still two hundred miles from the leprosarium which was our home. This trip was made by bus and as usual, the driver drove around the sharp mountain curves as if he were going to a fire. We hung on to our school bus-type seats to keep from sliding out of them and a little Bolivian boy on the seat behind us got sick. We won't go into further detail, but it suffices to say we had to pick up our hand baggage from the floor to save it from being saturated.

A big welcome awaited us at the colony but some big problems awaited us too. The Bolivian government had so consistently failed to provide funds for food and drugs that we were facing a real crisis in this area. Our mission buyer had allowed us to buy on credit -- that is, he was using money that was in other mission accounts to fill colony orders -- until a limit was reached in his ability to help us. We decided we could give free food only to those patients who were hospitalized. All others would have to purchase food from the colony store with their earnings from their little farms or other earnings. This created considerable unrest and a few patients who were chronic trouble makers became belligerent. Our field chairman, together with a couple of others, came to the colony and dismissed three men from the colony and put others on probation.

"Where would these men go?" That was their problem. There was another treatment center for leprosy in Bolivia, so we knew they could get medicine if they wanted it bad enough.

After a time, our mission office decided they would extend us credit for one more shipment of food. The money was sent to the city of Santa Cruz where a buyer for the mission purchased rice and other staples for the patients. Enroute to the colony, the truck hauling this cargo caught fire and all was burned. Some of the patients said, "This is God punishing us for our wickedness."

Finally, in August, we received funds from the government but what they sent only paid their obligation to us until the month of June which was already two months past. Also, there was very little left after we paid our debts to the mission. Nevertheless, we put all patients on some free food but at the same time told them that a certain amount of free work would be required of all.

At about this time, we received word from the Clarksville Bible church that our Chevrolet Carryall and baggage was soon to be shipped. This rejoiced our hearts because we needed the carryall badly. Myron and I were walking about four miles a day just to and from our work and there were always hauling jobs to be done.

Because of interstate shipping regulations and other factors, what this cost the Clarksville people in work and sacrifice is a story in itself. It also required Myron and our mission representative to the Bolivian government, to make a trip to La Paz.

Myron tells the story. "Unless we obtained a "customs liberation" we would have to pay one hundred percent duty on the Carryall and perhaps duty on our other baggage as well. La Paz at thirteen thousand foot elevation was dry and cold as usual. We wore our topcoats inside our unheated hotel rooms as much as we wore them outside. The Lord granted us favor with certain officials however, and we left La Paz with the liberation, some drugs for the colony and a promise of fifteen cots and materials for installing running water in the hospital. And who do you think one of the officials was? My predecessor as director of the colony who was dismissed for corrupt practices."

After their trip to La Paz, Myron contacted a doctor in Cochabamba who confirmed what he had suspected. He had developed a hernia from lifting packing boxes, barrels of kerosene and other heavy items and would have to undergo surgery. He returned to the colony first, however, to arrange for a temporary replacement.

Thanks to the Paul Masons and the Les Thompsons, our fellow workers in the colony, we were both able to go to Cochabamba for Myron's surgery. The cost for everything? About two hundred dollars in United States money. The surgery took place on October ninth, 1961.

This was not to be the end of major operations for the Gess family, however. On October twenty-third we received word by means of our Mission's radio communications that Priscilla was sick at school with vomiting and abdominal pains. It just "happened" that missionaries of another mission were enroute to Cochabamba from the school so they made a bed for Priscilla in the back of their pickup. Since we were still without an automobile, Paul Mason kindly took me to Cochabamba later. There was political trouble in Bolivia so we all prayed that there would be no trouble getting through the road blocks that certain groups had set up. There was no trouble and I arrived in Cochabamba that same night, just before Priscilla was to enter the operating room. The doctor said that in eight more hours the appendix would have burst.

Priscilla had barely returned to her studies when we again received word from the school that David was quite sick and that both he and Paul were on the bus enroute to Cochabamba. Paul would have been seventeen at the time and David fourteen. This time the doctor diagnosed the problem as epigastric hernia. But he said that while operating he would also do exploratory surgery in the area of the appendix. You can imagine that all of these medical problems were hitting us pretty hard financially even though medical costs were, at the time, much lower in Bolivia than in the States. But, the Lord is faithful, and this is where staff and students at the mission school stepped in with their gifts to help out so that David also could have the surgery he needed. Myron continues telling the story. "I was not yet carrying a full schedule of work following my operation, so it was decided that I should go to be with David, and allow Paul to return to school. So, on November fourth, David underwent surgery. In those days it was essential that someone accompany the patients night and day and hospitals provided an extra cot in the patient's room for the attending relative or friend. In as much as there was no recovery room at the hospital, I watched David carefully following the operation. However, I didn't think to check the hot water bottle the nurse had put at his feet. In the middle of the night, David called to me saying, "Daddy, my feet feel prickly." Upon checking I was shocked to find the nurse had put such hot water next to the bottom of David's feet that they were blistered. Well, the doctor gave the nurse a good scolding but the injury had been inflicted. In his days of recovery, David suffered more from the burned feet than he did in the surgery and to this day at times, still experiences a sensitivity in the area of the burns. So, after three major surgeries within one month, we hoped things would go more smoothly for us."

There was a time when it seemed that members of our staff were falsely accused for saying that a fellow from a family in an isolated area near the colony had entered one of patient's houses with the intent of stealing. The result was that one day about eight male outsiders, some half-drunk, ganged up on our coworker. He was really scared for awhile but eventually the whole thing "blew over" and no one was harmed. It's interesting that the verse on our Scripture calendar for that day was, "I will surely deliver thee, and thou shalt not fall by the sword." Jeremiah 39:18. Later, local authorities discovered that one of our expatients was the thief.

Anyone who has never lived outside the United States cannot fully appreciate what a privilege is his to merely drive to a shopping center and buy what he wants, providing he has the money, of course. A missionary cannot do this because many items are not available in the country in which he works or if they are available they cost two or three times as much as they would in the States. Therefore, the missionary must ship some things overseas. But getting baggage safely to its destination can be another story.

Now what about our new Chevy Carryall and the twenty- five pieces of baggage we had to leave behind in Clarksville when we flew back to Bolivia after our second furlough? Pastor Don Mathis of the Bible Church planned to drive the carryall and a farmer was going to haul the baggage on his truck to New York City. From there everything would be sent by ship to Peru and from there forwarded by rail to Bolivia. Such were the plans until interstate commerce regulations and other factors dictated otherwise.

Not knowing what else to do, our Clarksville friends consulted a fowarding agency in Grand Rapids who said they could ship the things but that all the boxes and barrels would have to be repackaged by them. I had done most of that packing. Because of previous experience I had filled all empty containers, such as canning jars, with smaller items and had used the rolled bandages for the leprosarium as packing material. In preparing a foam rubber mattress for shipping, Myron had first put sheets of formica next to it over which he secured sheets of plywood. The formica and plywood would eventually become kitchen cupboards---we hoped! Well, the forwarding agency removed all the bandages and put them in several large bales and used as filler a packing material that was of no use to us whatever as filler. Yet, shipping costs are calculated either by weight or volume, whichever is the most advantageous to the steamship line. The forwarding agency also saw fit to repack our mattress and in the process drove nails through the plywood into the formica which is almost priceless in Bolivia!

Although our Clarksville friends advised us that all had been shipped, we waited what seemed to be an eternity before they arrived. In the meantime the customs liberation on the Carryall had to be renewed twice and each occasion required a trip of about eight hundred miles round trip to the city of La Paz.

Myron recollects that on one of these trips, he received a small consolation in that he stood just a few feet from Prince Phillip of England when he passed by in an open car as a visiting dignitary to Bolivia.

Finally, in July of 1962, one year after our return to Bolivia, our Carryall and baggage arrived. But, we couldn't get it out of customs because in the meantime our liberation had once again expired. After another ten days of negotiating on Myron's part and another trip to La Paz with our field chairman, we were allowed to take possession of our things.

Even this, after so long a wait, was not pure joy. Upon examination we found the carryall to be badly dented in at least six different places, evidently by the cables used in lifting it. The headlights were broken and the windshield cracked. Even the glove compartment had been broken into. David had anchored a wood box of "boyish" treasures by chaining to the front seat. All the contents of that box were missing. Little by little as we unpacked the boxes and barrels we found many items missing from them. Fortunately, our insurance covered some of the loss, but some items were irreplaceable. Often things are stolen while they are in customs but if we protest the officials will likely give us a harder time and charge us more duty when the next shipment arrives!

So, dear fellow American, rejoice in the fact that as you select and purchase you can be reasonably sure that your purchase will be turned over to you promptly and in satisfactory condition. We knew that although these things were to be used mostly in the hospital and for other needs of the patients, we couldn't dwell on our loss. The Lord had allowed this to happen, and we accepted it as his will.

Among those times of discouragement, the Lord always had something with which to encourage our hearts. How faithful He is!

The New Chapel

❖

Chapter 10

Our devotional times, along with Bible study times, and Sunday services were all held outside under a big tree. It wasn't the best arrangement, especially during rainy season, but we didn't miss any meetings.

However, it was the patients' idea to start building a chapel. How big should it be? Could we afford the materials that would be needed for the building? Oh, so many thoughts went through our minds at that time. But God was in it! He provided funds designated especially for the chapel. The patients who could work did the work, and soon after the hospital was finished, the chapel was also finished. What a blessing it was! They also made rough, backless benches out of the lumber available and then to show their concern and love for us, made other benches with one rung of lumber for the back rest -- especially for the missionaries and their families. No patient would be allowed to sit on these. These rules were made by the patients themselves. God was bringing encouragement. It was a building where meetings could be held in spite of the rain. There were only openings for the windows, and the floor was mud. Sure, when the wind and rain blew, it blew in to some extent, but because the chapel had been built under three or four large trees, it was adequate. I can still hear some of the testimonies that our believers gave in that chapel. Their hearts were filled with gratitude for the privilege they had of hearing the gospel.

It was Easter time, and we had invited Bud and Frieda Garmo to spend the weekend with us. It was a perfect time for a dedication service. The believers were also invited from Mataral to join us in the services that Sunday morning. A baptismal service was also planned for that same afternoon. We had several very special numbers in song by Bud Garmo.

It had rained the night before Easter Sunday, making the river which runs through the colony property, higher than usual. The current was strong and Myron and Dr. White who were doing the baptizing had trouble keeping their balance. There were twelve persons baptized that afternoon. Four new believers from Mataral and eight were from the colony. It was thrilling to hear these give their testimonies of God's saving grace. Surely the Lord has been good, and God always seemed to give the encouragement just when we needed it most.

Easter was over and the Garmo family had returned to their work in Cochabamba. I had just come home from a rather trying day at the hospital. We were about to sit down to supper when we heard another truck stop outside our home. Sometimes our hearts cringed when we heard the sound of these motors. Invariably there was another new patient and this was the case this time as well.

Two men who had been riding in the cab came to the house saying, "We have a sick boy on the back of the truck! What shall we do with him?"

After examining Ricardo, right there on the truck, we realized he indeed was very sick and couldn't walk. So we transferred him to the back of our Jeep Station Wagon and took him to the colony. I planned to stay with him for a while; Myron would come and pick me up later. As vital signs were taken, I realized that this boy didn't have long to live on this earth. There was nothing I could do for him! No, nothing in a medical way, but I started sharing the gospel with him. At first there was no response. I continued reading scripture from my Spanish Bible and making a few comments. After some time, Ricardo opened his eyes and looked directly at me.

"Senora, is it too late for me to receive the Lord as my Saviour? I have done a lot of bad things and yet the Bible verse you read to me says that God loves sinners, will you tell me how I can ask Jesus to save me?" Tears came to my eyes as once again I saw a young man, just nineteen years of age, pass from darkness to light. A radiant smile came across Ricardo's face, and in a few minutes he had passed into eternity.

"Thank you Lord," I prayed, "Thank you for giving this dear young person the opportunity to accept you as Saviour. Lord, the next time I'm ready to "quit", please remind me of this night when Ricardo came to know YOU."

§ § §

One of the difficult but necessary experiences in missionary life is frequent separations from one's children. Usually missionary children not only must live at a boarding school, often several hundreds of miles from their parents, but the time eventually comes when they must leave the field and return to the United States for advanced schooling. Our eldest son Paul had graduated from high school, so we were to have the experience of sending our first-born home in August of 1962. We took him to the Cochabamba International Airport and rather tearfully saw him off to face life on his own. Yet, he was not alone because not only was the Lord with him but there were dear Christian friends back in Michigan who were to take him under their wings. They would help him get situated at the Grand Rapids School of the Bible and Music. Twice more in the future would we send a child home and in another case leave a child after furlough. On one such occasion when Priscilla, our youngest, was about to leave us we tried to console ourselves by telling her, "You know, if we didn't have these difficult times of separation, we would never have those glorious reunions that we all look forward to." And this is true. There is a price to pay for almost everything of real value in life and this is the cost a missionary family is willing to pay in order that the gospel might be taken to the remote areas of the world. There are people dying without any knowledge of the Saviour. It is a very small price to pay in the light of what HE paid that we might have everlasting life.

§ § §

Some of our new patients professed to know the Lord when they arrived. Myron had a devotional time and Bible Study with the entire group each morning before activities of the day began.

New babies who were born in the colony were immediately separated from their mothers and it was the time consuming job of Neva Miller to care for these babies. Was it cruel to separate these children from their mothers? Of course the idea was to protect them from contracting the disease. As strange as it may seem, the mothers never objected. In fact they were glad to give them up to be cared for in a way that they could not begin to provide for them themselves.

One day a man was brought to us in critical condition by two Roman Catholic priests. In addition to having leprosy in its advanced stages, this man also had an obstruction of the intestine. To remedy his condition Dr. White chose to operate, but this time surgery was done in the little adobe house we were then using for a hospital. A sheet was suspended over the operating table to catch any particle of dust and dirt that might fall from the tile roof. During the two nights following, Marge and I took turns going on duty to care for this man. Regular day-time schedules had to be continued. The third night, Dr. White offered to go "on duty". Marge and I were almost exhausted! That night the patient died.

There were some pleasant times in the colony however, as when some one got married or had a birthday. One morning, Myron and I went to the colony as usual in time for our morning Bible study together with the patients. We were surprised to see them all gathered together under the big tree waiting for us when we got there. Excitement seemed to hover in the air. Then one of the ladies, a patient named Blanca, stood up and said, "Don Mario, we have a program prepared this morning especially for the Senora Catalina (my name in Spanish). We know it is her birthday." Blanca was well qualified to do this sort of thing because she was the widow of a former army captain and was better educated than most of her fellow patients. There were special numbers in song, testimonies and a message from the Bible. I was surrounded by bouquets and later presented with gifts of handmade doilies, chickens, eggs, and a parrot.

Myron tells what happened on his birthday a couple of months later, "I was awakened at midnight by a group of patients who had come to sing Happy Birthday to me and who continued to sing several hymns and finally terminated with a prayer for God's blessing on me. The next day, I too was honored with a special program and gifts of flowers, chickens, and eggs." Such love touched our hearts for we knew that these people had not given out of their abundance, but out of affliction and deep poverty.

Decision making was also a big part of the work of the colony. Myron speaks: "It was good to have companions in the work, not only to share some of the physical burden, but to help in the decision making. Most discipline problems -- and there were many -- were left for me to handle except in a few cases where I selected several patients to evaluate a problem and determine the punishment, if any was in order. One such case involved a man named Juan, whom I had appointed storekeeper, and a young man named Benedicto stabbed Juan in the shoulder. After bringing Benedicto to trial, the "jury" decided that Benedicto should relinquish both his knife and pistol and spend each night in "jail" until Juan's wound was healed. The colony 'jail', which was constructed before our time, consisted of a cavity about the size of an outhouse carved out of a former river bank with a door of sheet metal. Later, the jury took pity on Benedicto and instead of putting him in jail each night required him to pay Juan the wages he lost as store keeper until his wound was healed.

Myron also devoted considerable time to problems evolving from love affairs and marriage.

For example, there arrived in the colony a handsome young man named German Paneagua whose name when translated to English becomes Herman bread-and-water. German fell in love with a young lady patient named Laura. However, a married woman in the colony, who had had a previous alliance with him, still had her eye on him. She wrote an insulting letter to Laura in an effort to thwart a marriage between the two. This led to a fight between German and the woman's husband. In the end, German and Laura married but after a few weeks Laura refused to live with him and nothing or no one could persuade her to do so. A consequence of this brief marriage was the birth of a baby girl who was adopted by missionaries and later married one of our M.K.'s (missionary kids). This couple spent several years serving in Brazil. Three other children were adopted and are now living in the United States.

Thus, life went on in the colony with many victories but also some defeats in our efforts to demonstrate and teach the Word of God. In a sense it was as if we were working with children; teaching, but also sometimes punishing.

One afternoon in April about two years after we had taken over the work of the colony, Myron and I went as usual to the "hospital" to do the afternoon's work. We were surprised upon arrival there to find the Bolivian Minister of Health and two other health officials. They had spent just enough time for two or three patients to tell them several untruths about how badly they were being treated, how they had to buy even salt for their food, etc. Later, however, several other patients told them that those people were lying and that they had never been better treated, not even in the hospital in La Paz.

We took our visitors on a tour of the colony showing them the pure bred hogs (purchased by missionaries) the good corn harvest, The lepers' houses, the babies being cared for by the Millers and many other things. After this we invited them to our house for cake and coffee. They were very pleasant to visit with. Following this they gave gifts of money to two men and their wives with which to start life outside the colony since in their cases the disease had now been arrested sufficiently for them to leave. Just before leaving, and before promising to return on May second to have dinner with us, the Minister removed his hat, shook our hands and said, "I can only thank you in the name of my country."

On May second, in anticipation of another visit from the Minister and his partners, I prepared an elaborate meal, and the patients prepared a special program in the Minister's honor. But the day passed with never a sight of our distinguished visitors. It left us all with a rather "let-down" feeling!

However, in late October, the minister, his wife and some lesser officials again arrived unannounced. As before the Minister seemed well-pleased with conditions in the colony and brought gifts of soccer uniforms, soccer balls, color books and crayons for the children and some medicines. He also promised twenty beds for the new hospital we were building, furniture and equipment for an office for Dr. White, and a new sewing machine for the lepers. After he finished speaking, one of the lepers boldly exhorted him, "Now, don't forget your promise!" The patient not only spoke advisedly but prophetically as well, because, as we recall, we never received the items that were promised."

We shall never forget, however, the obvious impression that the patients made on the Minister and his wife that day. For example, they sang a chorus entitled, "Alla en Los Cielos" which roughly translated means, "Over there in Heaven" and relates that in heaven we will no longer have trials, sick bodies, etc. Following this, Blanca the widow of the former army captain with her black eyes sparkling in a face distorted by leprosy, testified, "We may have lost our homes, our money and our health, but in coming here we have gained salvation and that is worth far more!" Upon hearing this, the minister's wife began to weep and hid herself behind their automobile.

Speaking of Blanca, reminds me that shortly after this she became quite ill and thought she was going to die. So, she sent for Myron to ask how she should go about making a will. A few hours later she gave Myron the finished document. In the distribution of her possessions she had willed to Ed Miller her six ducks! Now, although Ed had been a chicken rancher, he didn't like ducks at all. But it didn't matter anyway because Blanca didn't die then but instead left the colony several years later with her disease arrested.

One of the things impressed upon our hearts as we worked in the colony was the terrible stigma accompanying the disease of leprosy, at least in Bolivia. For example, there was the case of a leper brought to us from the city of Cochabamba by his relatives. We had received word several days earlier that he would be coming and that he would be coming in a special bus. He was brought to us in a bus, a little city bus owned by his relatives, but the man was dead upon arrival. He was filled with worms and the stench was terrible. There was nothing to do but bury him as quickly as possible. The thing that seemed so heartless to us was that the man's wife and other relatives wouldn't even stay for the funeral. Instead they asked for some disinfectant with which to wash their hands and the inside of the bus, and then left.

I also think of the man who was brought to us from the general hospital in the city of Santa Cruz. A large hospital truck came, but the man was not brought in the truck but rather in a small trailer hitched to the back of the truck! He had been very much uncared for and he told us that he doctor had suggested that he just be put out on the streets to die.

There was also a dear lady by the name of Encarnacion who was rather new in the colony. Through carelessness -- and not reporting for treatment -- she allowed flies to lay their eggs on her ulcerated hand. As a consequence her hand became filled with worms, and gangrene set in. I knew that an amputation might be required but our own medical doctor was outside the country. Therefore, Myron contacted our mission buyer in Santa Cruz by short wave radio. He suggested he ask the director of the health department if they could do something for the woman if we brought her to the city. He assured us that something could be done. Since this word didn't reach us until nine thirty in the evening, we readied the patient and our Jeep Station Wagon for a trip to Santa Cruz yet that night. Fortunately the Jeep ran well for a change and we made the seventy-five mile trip over rough mountain roads without difficulty. After three hours of sleep and a quick breakfast, we took the woman to the hospital but only encountered such responses as "Don't mention the word leprosy here. If people heard it they would never enter the hospital again!" One doctor said, "We could never place that woman on an operating table in the hospital!" Even the Director of Health went back on his word and said, "Instead, we will send a doctor back with you to do the surgery in your own hospital." So, after another arduous trip back to the leprosarium the "doctor" (only one in training) did the surgery with my assistance, amputating the lower arm. She lived, and the stump healed up nicely. These were people with whom we had opportunity to share God's Word. Later this woman also received the Lord as her personal Saviour. I believe she learned her lesson about not reporting for daily treatments.

But I think we were most affected by the behavior of a young man who was a student at a well-known Bible school in the city of Cochabamba. He had a sister, a fine Christian who was one of our patients. One day the young man, along with several other young people from the Bible Institute, came to hold a service for the patients. The sister had waited with great anticipation to see her brother once again. She saw him, but he never acknowledged her as his sister. She was heartborken and momentarily our hearts were filled with condemnation for the young man. What would we have done? Before we decide, let us consider that because of ignorance concerning leprosy, to have acknowledged that we had a sister with the disease, might have cost us our friendship with fellow students and possibly even a place of public ministry for the Lord.

Although days were busy and full, we continued to have a ministry in neighboring towns, visiting the church in Mataral where we had lived prior to moving to the colony. The church there needed encouragement and help. Bible studies were also held in different homes outside the colony. What a joy it was to see the eagerness of these people to hear the Word.

Encouragement And Changes

Chapter 11

At about the same time that Paul returned to the States, we finally received a small sum of money from the Bolivian government for the work at the leprosarium. It was the first money we had received from them in almost a year. They had given us some help in the form of a few pieces of machinery. With the help of some Peace Corps workers, a water system was installed for the hospital.

Although these improvements were helpful and appreciated, one cannot meet all the needs of lepers without money. So Myron protested by sending a telegram to the Bolivian Minister of Health, (compared in status to a member of the President's cabinet in the United States) stating that he refused to receive any more patients until he received more funds. Of course, such a statement didn't exactly please him. Myron wouldn't have been quite so blunt or bold had our previous more tactful approach brought results.

It was at this time that the United States Peace Corps was making quite a thrust in Bolivia and they offered to take over the leprosarium if we didn't want to continue.

In fact, a young man from the Peace Corps, just fresh out of college, visited us one day and while seated in our living room said to us, "You just don't know how to handle things here." Of course we should have recognized that when one has finished college he does have all the answers! To make a long story short, because our medical doctor had gone into another type of work and because all of us in the mission felt we could no longer continue the work under the burden we had been carrying, we severed our contract with the Bolivian Health Department.

There were many heart-rending experiences as we turned the work over to the Peace Corps. One was leaving behind our house, gardens, etc. which represented the work of seven years and this without any financial remuneration because everything was on government property. Photographers from a well-known American magazine came to take pictures of the new staff and later a rather condescending article by the new director appeared in another American magazine. It was a good thing we had endeavored to work not for the commendation of man, but for the glory of God. It is interesting, however, that even the new director and his associates didn't have quite all the answers because after two years they left the work again in the hands of the Bolivian government.

Incidentally, the Paul Masons stayed on for many years in the same area. They ministered to the spiritual needs of the few remaining patients and those outside the colony along with their dental needs. Dr. John White, now a doctor of psychiatry in western Canada, is a frequent contributor to Christian periodicals and the author of several books.

The leprosarium as such no longer exists, partly because the method of treating Hansen's disease has changed. Only the very worst cases are confined to a treatment center or Rehabilitation Center in the city of Santa Cruz. Others were allowed to take medication in their homes. Still there were fifteen of the "beyond hope" cases who were left in the colony to die! It was with these few remaining patients the Paul Masons had opportunity to minister.

Not only was it hard to leave our home at the leprosarium, it was hard to leave the patients, also. There were some trouble makers, of course, of whom three, we understand, were promptly dismissed by the Peace Corps. But most of them knew we had done the best we could for them and talked of presenting a petition to the Minister of Health asking us to stay. We believed it was best that we go, however, and we began to seek the Lord's will as to where we should work Since our Chevy Carryall was not an off-the-road vehicle, we wondered if there might be a village somewhere along the "highway" still unreached with the Gospel. A lengthy survey trip revealed that there were none truly unreached. We realized anew at this point that missionaries usually locate first in the cities, then in the villages and finally begin to reach out to the remotely located farmers and the tribal people. Why? Because this is the order of accessibility and comfort. One can usually obtain better food and housing in the cities and villages as well as medical help. Christian fellowship is also more readily available. This is why there are still many tribes in the world without the message of salvation.

We were then approached by both our field chairman and the

director of our school for missionary children to consider joining the staff there at our mission school. Although we appreciated so much the training being given our own children at the school, we had never given thought to working there ourselves. We had never trained to be school teachers although we had received considerable instruction in the principles of teaching. Then too being surrounded constantly by one hundred children, plus eating in a school dining room, wasn't particularly attractive. However, we knew we must put personal preferences aside and do what the Lord wanted us to do. After we had spent considerable time in prayer, it became clear to us that Tambo, where our school for missionary children is located, was where we should be.

Our home would be the little boys' dormitory. The dorm building consisted of ten rooms, and housed somewhere between twenty-five and thirty boys plus ourselves. In other words, we were dorm parents to all the boys in grades one through eight. Our private quarters consisted of one bedroom. It really wasn't all that private either. On one side there were double doors opening into the largest of the dormitory rooms. The smallest of the boys slept here. A door on the opposite side leading into the living room was the bedroom for the older boys.

Being parents to the many boys was almost a full-time job in itself, but this, by no means, was the extent of our responsibilities. Myron was to assist the director in the business realm of the school which included doing the bookkeeping, and in addition, participating in the gospel ministry to the Bolivians in the surrounding area.

I became the school nurse and teacher of piano. This was by no means the extent of our jobs at the school. There were more to follow.

There is one thing you learn immediately as a new dorm supervisor. The former supervisor was much better than you! Formerly, according to those dear little boys, they were allowed to do things that we didn't approve of. You listen and perhaps give a little here and there until you are quite sure that those same little boys may have forgotten or may be stretching the truth a bit.

"Here, Johnny, since you're a first grader and new at the school, I'll help you make your bed for the first couple of days."

"Billy, did you do a good job sweeping."

"David, remember it's your week to empty the waste baskets."

"Benny, do you have a clean handkerchief?" I asked, when getting the boys ready for our Sunday morning service. "Sure, Mrs. Gess, lots of them!" as he proceeded to pull several dirty ones from his pockets.

"Rick, do you have a comb?" "No, I don't need one. I have a butch!"

We soon saw that these boys make life interesting.

Chapter 11

There is a river at Tambo which is shallow enough for bathing much of the year. One Saturday afternoon Myron thought he would take fifteen of the smaller boys to the river. They could bathe in the river instead of taking a shower at the dorm and Myron thought he could relax a bit at the same time. He learned differently and tells the story: "What with seeing they didn't lose their towels and their wash cloths, didn't drop the soap in the sand, didn't fight, didn't go out too far -- there was no relaxing for me! Then, there was the long walk back to the dorm with each boy trying to carry his own weight in pretty stones he had found at the river."

As I look back now, I wonder who learned the most at Tambo--the kids or the dorm parents. Inasmuch as our dorm was made up of boys ranging in ages from seven to fourteen, it was necessary to schedule bedtimes according to the boys' ages. Since a day began early for everyone in Tambo, the little boys in grades one through four were required to come in from their play at six thirty in the evening, take showers, brush their teeth and have a devotional time with either Myron or me before the bigger boys in grades five through eight came in from study hall at seven thirty for a similar routine before going to bed.

I recall a few incidents from these evening hours that are worth remembering.

Some of these have to do with a boy named little Stevie. He was slower than the proverbial "molasses in January" but likable nevertheless. One evening all the little boys were doing a pretty good job of brushing their teeth and taking their showers in the bathroom which was a separate adobe block building behind the dorm. Then Myron noticed that Stevie was missing. Myron returned to the dorm and found Stevie stretched across his bed with all his clothes off except for his long sleeved shirt, which was still tightly buttoned around his right wrist and pulled down over his hand. Myron was about to give him a "tongue lashing" about his being so slow when he said, "Of course, Mr. Gess, I couldn't get it unbuttoned; I had only one hand to work with."

Myron tells of another incident--this time with Stevie. All the boys had finished their showers and were ready to have devotions except Stevie who still didn't have his pajamas on, I said, "You get your pajamas on Stevie, and I'll hang up your towel and wash cloth." His response was, "You're a good man, Mr. Gess. My Dad would have said, 'Put your pajamas on and hang up your towel and wash cloth too'."

I remember another incident with Stevie that took place one afternoon just outside the bathroom as I was giving one of the older boys instructions as to how he should perform his newly assigned task. You know, many times it would have been far easier to do the work detail ourselves than to see that some boy did it, but that would not have taught faithfulness to duty. At any rate, after I had spent considerable time telling the boy just how he should go about cleaning the bathroom, little Stevie, who had been standing by listening, looked up at me and asked, "Mrs. Gess, don't you ever do anything around here?" It's a good thing I didn't follow my natural inclinations after that remark! We remained good friends, however, and a few years ago it was Myron's privilege to teach him at our Bible Institute in Waukesha, Wisconsin.

One evening Myron having the boys' devotions, tells of another incident; "I recall reading to the boys one evening from the book of Genesis the account of Adam and Eve's fall. Afterward, as I tried to impress upon the boys the seriousness of their error in partaking of the forbidden fruit, one smart little fellow said, 'Well, Mr. Gess, I don't think what they did was all that bad. They could have taken two apples instead of just one!' Now, whether this was truly his evaluation of Adam and Eve's deed, I'm not sure, but it is interesting that this fellow gave us trouble throughout most of his years at Tambo and, as far as we know, today, as an adult, is not walking with the Lord."

As would be expected, sometimes our big family tested our patience and endurance but there were those rewarding moments too. One such came one evening while we were gathered in the living room listening to some music. An affectionate little fellow named Johnny, with his arm around my neck, whispered, 'Tommy says, "The Gesses are people who have a heart for little boys'." Maybe the fudge I had made had something to do with it.

Can you imagine how hard it would be to keep a dormitory and twenty-seven little boys clean when it rains three days in a row and the ground surrounding the dormitory is red clay? The boys needed to go from one building to another for classes, and there was no gymnasium in which they could play. Neither was there a provision for washing and drying clothes except wringer washers and outdoor clothes lines. This is what can be expected anytime during the months of November through February which are the warmest and wettest months in Bolivia.

Because of the rains it is more difficult to get to the off the highway villages. Yet, on weekends these are the places to which some of our high school boys and some staff endeavored to go to have a ministry with the villagers and country folk.

One Friday afternoon Myron endeavored to take our son David and two other boys to the village only to find a river far too high to cross with our Carryall. They tried again the following morning and had to be pulled out by a four wheel drive vehicle.

After that, when these fellows wanted to go out on a weekend ministry and witnessing trip, which they did quite often, they hitched a ride on a truck that was going their way.

Sometimes we returned to the leprosarium or the village of Mataral for meetings in which Myron usually shared the Word. I played the marimba and our daughter Ruth, the accordion. Although the believers were very poor, they were so grateful for our visits. Out of their poverty, they often served us bread and coffee or gave us a gift of produce from their gardens.

Not every Sunday was free for such excursions, however. As a staff, we took turns cooking on Sundays in order to give our regular cook a day off. Even the men took turns with the help of two or three high school girls. Myron had never had occasion to cook for one hundred people before so he was very happy that Ruth was one of his helpers. Both Ruth and Priscilla learned how to cook when they were home from school on vacations. Even then, one Sunday when Myron and the girls were cooking they got a little too much pepper on the meat, but everyone accepted it good-naturedly. After all, we were cooking in South America where everything is highly seasoned!

Time passes quickly at Tambo, and before we knew it, it was the month of May and time for graduation services. Because most parents live hundreds of miles from the school, about the only time they can observe their children in programs is at graduations. So, we usually have three days of activities. There are choral numbers by both junior and senior choirs, piano recitals and plays by all age categories. Sometimes as many as one hundred guests arrive. Lodging of some kind for all must be arranged. It's a great time for all and the climax is the graduation service with a guest speaker plus speeches by outstanding students and the giving of awards for special merit. We expressed gratitude to God for His goodness as Priscilla spoke for the eighth grade graduates and was given the citizenship or good conduct award. Ruth spoke for the seniors. For the second year in succession, Ruth was also given the citizenship or good conduct award.

It was a very sad day when once again we had to say good-bye to the second one of our children. A few weeks later we saw Ruth off to the United States to join Paul at the Grand Rapids School of Bible and Music.

I believe this is one of the hardest things a missionary has to face on the foreign field. It is one thing to see them off to a missionary boarding school where we would not see them for several months, but another thing to send them off so many miles to face the world without Mom and Dad. What a blessing and comfort it was to know that each one had received the Lord Jesus as their Saviour before they left home. We knew HE would be with them.

Chapter 11

We, of course, eagerly awaited each letter from Paul or Ruth telling us how things were going with them. Since Ruth is less outgoing in personality than Paul, she found adjustments to life in the States a little more difficult than Paul did. However, they both found the Lord sufficient in every area of their lives. Because they had to work their way through school, they found employment with the Zondervan Company where they still have many friends. After a time one of the managers wrote to us telling us they were well satisfied with Paul and Ruth's work and that with Paul as an employee they were saving considerable money on step ladders! -- Paul was about six feet, six inches tall at that time.

An Early Christmas Vacation

Chapter 12

Both the curriculum and vacation periods at our school in Bolivia correspond closely with those of schools in the United States, so that children either going home on furlough or returning from furlough can make the transition without too much difficulty. There is one difference, however. In Bolivia the children complete nine months work in eight so that they may have a longer vacation with their parents at the Christmas break.

A vacation period is not a period of inactivity for the staff. We, for example, used the months of May to August to completely redecorate our dorm. This included repairing the cloth ceilings in almost every room, as they had begun to fall down because of leaks in the roof.

Our school director, David Lotz, and his family, used a portion of the vacation to visit Mrs. Lotz's family members, who were missionaries in Brazil. Almost immediately upon their return, Mr. Lotz became ill with infectious hepatitis. Mrs. Lotz and a daughter took sick soon after. My duties as school nurse increased immediately. Myron's did as well as he assumed some of Mr. Lotz's responsibilities. We both became more involved with teaching also. I took on the course of home nursing in addition to piano and typing which I had taught previously. Myron began teaching high school English, I & II. At one time when Myron questioned his qualifications for teaching some things he had not formally studied beyond high school, our school director responded, "You probably do a better job than some teachers in the United States who do it only for a salary." Whether the qualifications were in hand or not, we must have taught our students something because in achievement tests they consistently ranked two years higher than the national average in the United States. The teaching-learning process took place in unpretentious adobe block buildings.

At one point in the course of events at the school, it was necessary for me to take some high school girls to the hospital in Cochabamba. I drove our carryall the one hundred and eighty mile one way trip, over a not too good highway with almost no towns or service stations along the way. The nature of the trip necessitated my being away for several days. This left Myron alone to tend to the boys of our dorm.

He writes: "Recognizing that I might be short on patience at such a time, I presume I was a little more lenient than usual. The boys in turn saw this as an opportunity to be quite lax in doing their chores quickly and well. This went on for about four days until one morning before classes began, I lined them all up and gave each a swat with a paddle as they walked by. The response in conduct was miraculous and I wished I had taken action sooner. A few minutes later when Joy inquired by our shortwave radio how things were going, I said, "Fine," and proceeded to tell her what I had just done. But she remembered what I had forgotten. All the mothers of those little boys would also be listening to the mission's radio communications and might be broken hearted as they visualized their child getting a spanking so early in the morning. However, we as a school had the full backing of parents that their children should be spanked if they needed it, and I felt no concern, and heard of no adverse reaction from the mothers."

Following that episode, however, Mrs. Garland, a temporary staff member, did give Myron some assistance in supervising the dorm until I returned.

As time went on, more and more people came down with hepatitis in spite of many efforts to kept the disease from spreading. By the middle of November when we had twenty-two students and two staff members sick, we decided to close the school. Most parents came for their children but some could not make the trip at that time so we continued to care for their children at the school. Both David and Priscilla had hepatitis and the doctor in Cochabamba concluded that I either had it or something very similar; and order a reduced schedule for me. From our standpoint it was good that school had closed for a lengthy Christmas vacation.

THE SUN SHINES AGAIN

We were rather pleasantly surprised that when school reopened in January of 1964 we had only fourteen boys to care for in our dormitory, in contrast to the twenty-some we had previously. This was good because it seemed as if I was making more frequent trips to Cochabamba with seriously sick students, which meant an increased work load for both of us. A high school girl named Joetta was one who had to be taken quickly because of acute appendicitis. However, one trip and one operation was not to bring an end to health problems because a second operation was required and eventually she had to be taken to the States for further treatment. One must remember that although doctors in some underdeveloped countries do the best they can, they are often seriously handicapped by the lack of training and sophisticated equipment such as we have here in the Untied States.

In April we were blessed by a week's ministry by Bill Gothard of the well known Bill Gothard seminars. It was an especially busy time as classes were held as usual but the Lord was able to do a work in many lives including that of our daughter Priscilla who had lacked the assurance of her salvation.

However, it seems that not all was done that could have been done in the hearts of a few of our high school boys, who had been giving us much concern. Some days later, in the middle of the night, we heard what we thought were gunshots. Afterward we learned that some high school boys had set off several firecrackers. We also found upon arising the next morning that the school's water supply had been shut off, the school bell taken down and many toilet seats had been covered with grease. Now, we could have regarded everything as non-malicious pranks except the greasing of the toilet seats. Since the grease the boys used was a dark lubrication grease, you can imagine what happened when several little boys from our dorm used the bathroom during the night or early in the morning. The grease first stained them, then their pajamas and finally their bed sheets as they crawled back into bed. Some of our staff were especially upset by what the high school boys had done because these pranks were just a few of a crescendo of mischievous acts by them. So, a meeting was held and it was decided that the boys' punishment should be one Saturday of hard labor without pay. I might add that the following month, the ringleader of the group had to be dismissed from the school for a continuing bad attitude and disrespect. In contrast, one of the other fellows saw the error of his way, graduated from our school with honors, did his college work in Canada, and is now back at the school as a member of the staff.

REACHING OUT

Well, another semester of school ended with three days of graduation activities at the end of May followed by our annual field conference. Both events were occasions of great blessing. At that conference, Myron was appointed interim director of the school until our permanent director returned from furlough. He was also elected vice president of the New Tribes Mission Corporation in Bolivia and was already serving as secretary of our Field Committee, which is the administrative body of the field. It was obvious that neither of us were going to be idle in the days and months ahead.

On another occasion early one Sunday morning, we drove to a rather remote village. Alice Mickelson was working there. She had invited us to come for the Sunday afternoon service. Alice, for many years, taught at Tambo but she was now serving alone in this national village. She made her home in a single room at the back of a Bolivian "tile factory". At about two thirty the people gathered and the meeting began. Now, Myron wasn't considered a long-winded preacher, and didn't preach long that afternoon, but the meeting continued for two and one-half hours. They were taking full advantage of our visit. Myron tells of one incident that greatly amused us both; "Is there any other man taller than you?" was the question put to me -- I'm six feet four inches tall, "Do you mean in Bolivia?" I asked the inquirer, "No in your country." My reply was, "Oh yes, my oldest son is taller than I." The man shook his head in disbelief.

A WELCOME CHANGE

It was summer in the year 1964. That is, it was summer in the United States, but winter in Bolivia, at which time we were to have the usual school vacation during the months of June, July and most of August. The vacation period would give us some opportunities for travel, both as part of our ministry and for personal reasons. This indeed was a welcome change.

Our first trip took us the nearly two hundred miles to the city of Cochabamba, where each family member visited the doctor, dentist and optometrist. Having taken care of these more essential matters, we returned toward Tambo; but at a point about one third of the way from Cochabamba, turned off on a less traveled road toward the beautiful city of Sucre. Sucre is considered the cultural center of Bolivia and is sometimes considered the capital although the president of Bolivia lives in La Paz, and all government business seems to be transacted there. Sucre is located at about ten thousand feet altitude. Our friends, Dr. and Mrs. Roger Brown, who made their home there, had invited us to visit them. Dr. Brown was awaiting us at the entrance to the city in order that he might guide us to their home about seven kilometers on the other side.

Dr. Brown, was a medical doctor from New Zealand. He and his wife, devoted most of their time to the evangelization of the colorful Quechua Indians, who populate the area outside the city, and to the translation of Scripture into the Quechua language. Although we were quite accustomed to the Quechua Indians living in the vicinity of Cochabamba, we had never before observed those in the area of Sucre. Two things about the men's mode of dress immediately caught our attention. First, they wore rather close-fitting black felt hats, almost like helmets, that were decorated with bright artificial flowers. Secondly, although their tight-fitting homespun pants were held up in the front in what we consider the normal position, the back of the pants actually passed below the buttocks. Nothing was exposed, however because they wore long shirts which in some miraculous way seemed to stay well tucked in. It seemed to us, however, a most dangerous way to wear one's trousers!

Dr. Brown did not spend a great deal of time in medical work but did dispense some medicines to the Indians. One afternoon he introduced Myron to an Indian woman who had come to him for help. As Myron grasped her hand he immediately sensed the claw-like form of a hand belonging to one who had leprosy. A bit later, Myron said to Dr. Brown -- in English, "I believe this lady has leprosy." "Do you really," replied Dr. Brown, "I've been treating her for rheumatoid arthritis." "Well," Myron said, "Why don't we call Joy and see what she thinks." It didn't take many looks to realize this lady did indeed have leprosy.

The following afternoon, Dr. and Mrs. Brown took us uptown to see the ornate churches and government buildings. As we sat in his pick up truck, Myron and I noticed a woman coming toward us with a bandaged hand carefully tucked beneath her shawl. We said "There's another one!" Later upon investigation, Dr. Brown found that there indeed were many lepers in that region but nothing was being done to help them. Sometime afterward, a treatment center for leprosy was established in that area.

Another trip that summer took us to the lowland city of Santa Cruz, where Myron asked the manager of the Parker Drilling Company, a company that normally drilled wells. We were hoping to have a well at the school. We knew that the silt-filled and contaminated river water, even after chlorination, was likely the cause of much illness at the school so he was eager to help. He named the day that his men and a drilling rig would come to the school to begin work. We prepared accordingly. The day came and went without our seeing any well-drillers. The next morning, on our radio communication, our mission buyer in Santa Cruz called Tambo and began to sing, "Noel, Noel (no-well, no-well)" and then proceeded to tell us that no pipe was available, therefore no well drillers would be coming. We were keenly disappointed but the humorous way in which the message was transmitted to us, softened the blow, and we understood better why many English speaking people outside our Mission said they wouldn't miss listening to our broadcasts for anything! At the present time our missionaries are required to transmit in Spanish so that the authorities can be sure they are not involved in some kind of subversive activity!

One Sunday afternoon toward the end of our school's summer vacation, we were called to the village of Mataral. One of the believers had given some land on which to build a church, and they, as a congregation, were about to begin the construction. Since Myron was the first to ever consistently preach the Word there, they thought he should lay the cornerstone. Although we ourselves weren't much for formalities and since the building was to be only a small structure of adobe blocks, the laying of a square field stone in one corner seemed almost ridiculous. However, these humble farm people had been called from darkness unto light and the construction of a church building was a meaningful step in the right direction for them. Juan, the leader of the group, took charge of the service with others helping, and we all sensed the presence and blessing of the Lord.

Today a small church still remains in Mataral. The Gospel continues to go forth. There is no residing missionary, but Juan is a faithful and zealous worker for the Lord.

A New Year Begins

Chapter 13

School began late in August with the usual hubbub of activity with students arriving from their homes and some staff members returning from vacation activities in other places in Bolivia. Our permanent director had not yet returned from furlough, so Myron was to continue as interim director with a newer staff member serving both as a teacher and principal of the grade school.

Myron writes: "What I am about to tell you of this individual, I tell you so that you may realize that not all who go to a foreign field qualify as missionaries. This person had been allowed to come to the field because we were rather desperate for qualified teachers at the school. She had not completed our missionary training course in the States and had not come to the spiritual maturity which is so necessary to a missionary whether he serves as evangelist, maintenance man, teacher or whatever. Consequently, the beginning of this new school year was the beginning of a period of heartaches for both her, and all of us on the staff."

"First of all, she was uncooperative in moving to a different dormitory from the one she had supervised the previous semester. The move was important in order for her proper function as a member of the staff. Her reason: She liked living where she was because it was close to the dining room. Secondly, she was uncooperative in helping to make important decisions. In fact, she didn't even bother to attend some of our staff meetings. Sometimes after a heart-rending decision such as a student's dismissal from school, she could be heard to say, "Well, I'm glad I didn't have a part in that!" Thirdly, she would deliberately break rules of the school such as walking on the patio grass which had to be coaxed into growing in that semi-arid part of Bolivia. Her reason: 'Such rules apply only to students, I'm a staff member!' Yet this person had been a principal of a small public school in the United States. We prayed for this individual and as an entire staff, endeavored to counsel her. Finally, I guess we just tolerated her until she eventually had to be asked to leave the work and the mission. This lady had many commendable qualities but she was lost to the work because of a stubborn and uncooperative spirit."

Is missionary life all roses? No, it just behooves us to have a very close walk with the Lord. We need to exercise spirit, of forgiveness as Christ also forgave us, who were so unworthy to become a child of God.

One highlight of the semester was a visit to the school by the American Ambassador to Bolivia, Mr. Henderson, and his wife. They had Sunday dinner with us and although we normally ate off plastic table coverings, I managed to scrounge up enough white table cloths for all the tables, even though some of the cloths were bed sheets. Some students provided special music. We found the Hendersons humble, amiable people; aren't most truly great people humble? They seemed impressed with our school. They were amazed that we had been able to construct certain buildings for only seven thousand dollars when elsewhere they were costing several times more. Of course our students wasted no time asking for autographs!

One would think that in a school for MK's or missionary kids, all would go well. Let's remember that students and staff alike all have the old nature within them, and we all, without exception, need a Saviour.

We already mentioned some of the problems the staff faced in this semester of school. This was not to be the end. We also had to dismiss three boys and one girl from our high school. They were all from Missions other than our own but they just as well could have been from ours. Dismissal creates problems for both the student and his parents. The student's education is interrupted and the parent's service for the Lord may be affected too. It is also a difficult experience for the director of a school to have to inform parents that this sort of action has been taken against their child. It was interesting to see how some of the parents reacted.

In the case of two of the boys, who were brothers, the father asked us to reconsider our final decision. Myron called a special meeting of the staff. They held to their previous decision which made the father very unhappy. He reminded us of what he had done for the school, etc. The father of the other boy said, "I'm in full accord with what you did. If you had not dismissed him I would have come and removed him anyway because of his problems."

At about this same time, we had a resignation in the general field administration, and Myron was selected to be interim field chairman until a permanent chairman returned from furlough. He wasn't eager for the position since he felt he already had enough responsibility and work, but agreed to do it. Myron mentioned in his journal that he could not forget how most of our fellow workers supported him with their encouragement and prayers. The reference in I Thessalonians 5:14 rang true. Both Myron and I were fainthearted as we realized the responsibility the Lord had given, but we were encouraged by the faithfulness of coworkers. So although faint, we continued to pursue, "pressing toward the mark for the prize of this high calling of God in Christ Jesus." (Philippians 3:14).

Another semester of school ended and we entered our month long Christmas vacation. I had not been well for some time and on a couple of occasions had to spend an entire week in bed. It seemed best that we go to Cochabamba where I could be under a doctor's care. My weakened condition persisted, so we spent Christmas day in Cochabamba instead of at home. Because of medical expenses we had very little to spend on gifts, but a day or two before Christmas a parcel arrived from Myron's sister Frances. It contained articles of clothing we needed badly. There were other goodies that could not be purchased in Bolivia at any price, so we did have a special treat.

Priscilla was with us throughout our stay in Cochabamba but David was invited to the Yuqui Indian work in the lowlands for a time. His biggest thrill was shooting several wild turkeys and catching a seventy-five pound fish. At about the same time, we were receiving letters from Paul and Ruth in the United States. Paul wrote about Marilyn," the most beautiful girl in the world" according to him, and Ruth wrote about a Dave Sommer who was six foot four inches tall, good-looking and played both the piano and organ. It was at times like these that we wished there had not been four thousand miles separating us from our children.

Myron writes again: "As the time for school approached for us to reopen and Joy still not feeling strong enough to take on her duties at Tambo, we wondered if the Lord might be directing us to move permanently to Cochabamba. The regular director of our school had not yet returned from furlough. He was due, however, before the opening day of school. I didn't want to shirk my responsibilities at Tambo, yet there was logic in making the move to Cochabamba. Other field leaders were at their respective posts, so the only way we could communicate was by radio. We were able to share facts and our feelings with one another. All thought it best that we relocate in Cochabamba. That decision seemed to be confirmed by the Lord a little later when we were back at Tambo packing and preparing for the move. In speaking with a Bolivian trucker about hauling our household goods to Cochabamba, he told me the cost would be equal to seventy United States dollars. That day we received two checks in the mail totaling exactly seventy dollars."

ANOTHER MOVE -- ANOTHER MINISTRY

In addition to my poor health, another factor that influenced our move to Cochabamba was Myron's need as interim field chairman to be able to travel throughout the field and be able to readily communicate with all the missionaries. This was usually possible from Cochabamba.

More from Myron's journal: "We were not long in Cochabamba before it became necessary for me to make a trip to the city of Guayaramarin. It is one of our most remote stations, located on the border between Bolivia and Brazil. A problem had arisen. Tom and Wanda Moreno had gone on furlough. Because there were no missionary substitutes, Tom left the work in the hands of two men who had been appointed as deacons in the church, and who had been trained in the teaching of the Word.

Tom felt they were capable of carrying on in his absence. There was another Mission working in this large town. During the Morenos absence, the believers were persuaded to become one group. One might think that no such problems should ever arise on a foreign field where the need is great, and the laborers so few, but they do.

Together with a representative of the other Mission, I traveled by plane to the city of Trinidad where we needed to spend the night before continuing to our destination. While in this town, I looked up relatives of one of our leprosy patients. They were overjoyed that I had gone to the trouble to visit them because they had wished to send a gift of money to their relative but wondered how they could safely do it. I was their answer. One thing impressed me, however, and that was the caution with which they talked about their relative, and her illness. I was instructed to lower my voice lest any outsider hear. They, like their relative, might be ostracized from society if word got around that there was leprosy in the family. The next day as we continued to fly to Guayaramarin, I was fascinated, as I had been the previous day, by what I saw beneath the plane. The land was extremely flat with many meandering rivers everywhere. Since it was the rainy season, many rivers had overflowed their banks creating vast lakes. Here and there a settlement could be seen where a rancher and his family braved the moisture, the heat, and insects and possible wild Indians as well, in order to make a living. I thought, 'How can cattle graze in such wet country?' Then I remembered that when the rainy season ended and the waters receded there would be abundant vegetation for the cattle to feed upon."

"Tom and Wanda Moreno who had returned from furlough had not received word that we were coming. As a result they were not at the airport to meet us, but gave us a warm welcome when we arrived at their door. That evening those of both Mission groups gathered to discuss our problems and endeavored to find a solution. Those of the other Mission stated that our believers felt uncared for during the Morenos' furlough and sought the fellowship and security of another group. Our national leaders had been made to feel that it would be better to have a foreign missionary teaching them. We, on the other hand, declared our feeling that they should not have assimilated our group into theirs without having first consulted us. The conclusion: We would let matters stand as they were and the Morenos would expend their energies in evangelizing others who were still unreached with the gospel. It is interesting that today we have the larger, more flourishing church with an outreach by both radio and by native evangelists. There is no further need of a foreign missionary in that city."

Myron returned to Cochabamba with a mountain of work awaiting him. In addition to his being interim field chairman, he was also bookkeeper for the entire field. He had hoped to continue keeping Tambo's books as well, but that proved impractical, and from the standpoint of time, impossible.

In the meantime, I continued in poor health with X-rays showing that my gall bladder was not functioning. Surgery was performed by a Bolivian doctor who had been trained in the United States. One of our missionary nurses was on hand to observe the operation. To the doctor's amazement, no gall bladder could be found! He called in other doctors to prove his point. Then he removed my appendix and closed the incision. Later in his office, and somewhat embarrassed, he showed us an article from the medical journals stating that one in ten or twenty thousand people are born without a gall bladder. Myron's comment, "I always knew my wife was a unique person!"

Good News From The Tribes

Chapter 14

All of us rejoiced in the month of March, 1965, when word was received through radio communications that our missionaries had made friendly contact with both the Yuqui and Toromono Indian tribes. The Yuqui roamed a portion of the wet lowlands in central Bolivia; whereas the Toromonos inhabited the jungle area of the northwest fairly close to the Peruvian border. Both tribes were savage. Sporadic warfare between the Yuqui and Bolivian nationals, had prevailed for some time, with the Bolivians shooting any Indian on sight. This, of course, made any friendly contact with them by our missionaries very difficult.

The procedure to reach each tribe had been as follows: Our men first penetrated the jungle in an attempt to discover the Indians' trails. Tracks, bent twigs, ashes from fires built by the Indians were evidence that the Indians had been there. It was on these trails that the missionaries left gifts of knives, machetes, large tin cans, pieces of brightly colored cloth --- anything that the Indians would find attractive and useful. From time to time our men would return to see if any gifts had been taken. If they had, they would leave other gifts. If the Indians had left a dead snake or an arrow in the trail pointed in the direction from which the missionaries would have come, that meant, "we don't want to be friends!" If, on the other hand, the Indians left nothing or if they left a gift of value, the missionaries assumed the Indians wished to be friends. Exchange of gifts continued over a period of years. There were long gaps of time when nothing happened. This usually indicated the Indians had grown fearful or had left the area in search of food elsewhere. At last a man to man contact was made. This was made with fear and trembling on the part of the Indians. Our men were trusting God for protection as well as to calm the Indians' fear of the white man. We all wished to see an encounter with no loss of life and a beginning of a friendly relationship.

Although one friendly contact usually meant continued success, this was not always true, in the case of the Yuqui. For example, following an earlier friendly contact in a different location, the Indians began to "rough house" with our men in a rather brutal way. At times they would throw our men to the ground and choke them almost to the point of death but would release their hold before the last moment arrived. Eventually, when one of the missionaries resisted an Indian, the Indian drew his bow and shot the missionary in the arm. The missionaries saw this as a prelude to worse things and no further contacts were made for a time. Then this friendly contact was made.

Later, a friendly contact was again experienced by our men. The Yuqui were as physically dirty as they were savage even though they lived right by the river. The Toromonos, on the other hand were a handsome, clean people. Our missionaries continue to work with both groups. Many have come to know the Lord, schools have been established and useful vocations such as agriculture are being introduced.

In the meantime, my health did not improve to any great extent and Bolivian doctors hinted about additional surgery. We did not look too favorably upon this, and especially having it take place in Bolivia. We were one year short of regular furlough time, but adjustments are sometimes made because of health or family needs. In a sense, at this time we also had a family need. Both Paul and Ruth had been away from us for some time and were eager to talk with us. While in Michigan, both had met prospective life partners. Ruth, especially, seemed to need our counsel in this matter. In times such as these, a missionary must decide which is his first responsibility, his children or the Lord's work. In this instance, as in some other instances we concluded that our children took priority. After all, if we lost our children through bitterness or lack of wisdom on their part, we alone might remain in the Lord's work. On the other hand, if we momentarily stepped aside to help our children, some day we might see them serving the Lord as well.

We began to pray and to plan. Our permanent field chairman, Dick Wyma and his wife, had returned from furlough and Dick had taken up his duties once again. His wife, Lucille, an experienced bookkeeper, was willing to take over that aspect of Myron's work. Thus, the Lord was preparing the way before us and Paul and Ruth were overjoyed at the prospect of seeing us within a couple of months.

I mentioned previously that Bolivia is a country of revolutions. In fact, someone has calculated that Bolivia has had, on the average, a revolution every other year since it's independence from Spain. One such disturbance erupted just at the time of our annual field conference at Tambo. Road blocks were set up by certain political groups, but, as the Lord would have it, they were removed at the time our missionaries had to travel to and from conference.

After conference, Priscilla, David, Myron and I accompanied by Carol Barton, one of our single lady missionaries, left Cochabamba for the United States. Our first flight by a Bolivian airline took us only as far as the capitol city of La Paz where we were to transfer to a United States airline. Our flight from La Paz was not scheduled until later that afternoon, but we refrained from going into the city because of the political conditions. The airport at La Paz is at an altitude of thirteen thousand feet and therefore is almost always cold. There were comfortable chairs and a fireplace in the waiting room. We did not mind waiting and relaxing.

The airport at La Paz is the world's highest commercial airport, and in the days before the runway was lengthened, propeller powered commercial planes were equipped with auxiliary jets to assist them in takeoff. Our takeoff went well although our flight was a little rough until we leveled off at about thirty thousand feet.

By late afternoon we were in Lima, Peru where we were put up in one of the finest hotels at the airline's expense. Even our meals were free, so we really "lived it up". Being in a lighthearted mood, we were glad our waiter had directed us to a rather secluded area of the very formal dining room. We shall never forget the dessert we chose. It was a half coconut filled with ice-cream and garnished with fruit and nuts.

The waiter had said when we ordered, "You'll never finish it!" and I think he was correct. As I reflect on this experience now, I am sobered by the thought that as we lived one night in the manner of Peru's wealthiest people. Not far from the hotel were hundreds of the world's poorest people. Probably they lived on an income of about one hundred dollars per year. Among them there were, without a doubt, many who were lost without the gospel. Following breakfast the next morning, everyone managed to get into the hotel's bus which was to take us to the airport. That is all except Myron and me. Consequently, we were driving in the hotel manager's rather ancient Cadillac, at a speed we didn't appreciate.

We had only brief stops at Quito, Ecuador and in Panama, before arriving in Miami. During the flight, David and Myron had an opportunity to witness for the Lord to a young Ecuadorian who was en route to a college in the United States.

One thing that impressed us upon arrival at Miami's International airport was the presence of so many Spanish- speaking people from Cuba. If it was that way in 1965 what must it be like now!

A friend in Miami assisted us in finding a good used car which we purchased, and immediately began our travels toward Michigan. We'll not go into detail about flat tires, faulty car jacks and other deficiencies that sometimes characterize a used car, but this one had it's share. The Lord undertook in every difficulty. After a few days we were in Grand Rapids at Zondervan's downtown bookstore where Paul, Ruth and Dave Sommer, Ruth's fiancee were employed. You can imagine the glorious reunion that took place in that store! I think the other Zondervan employees were almost as excited as we were!

Paul graduated from the Grand Rapids School of Bible and Music that evening and many relatives and friends were on hand for the occasion. Mr. Miles, the president of the school, made mention of our arrival from Bolivia as he handed Paul his diploma. Like the pleasure of seeing sunshine after rain, one cannot really experience all the joys of reunion unless he has also experienced the pain of separation.

A few days later while visiting near Clarksville, we had the privilege of meeting Paul's friend, Marilyn Rose. We found her to be a lovely girl indeed, and looked forward to the day when she might become one of our family.

A Furlough Ministry

Chapter 15

We knew when we came home on furlough in 1965 that we would be serving on the staff at one of our training institutes, but we did not know which one. While we were waiting for that decision to be made by our mission's leaders, we were thankful for a temporary home on Myron's brother's farm near Niles, Michigan. The tenement house he made available to us was not luxurious but was clean and adequate and because of numerous meetings in churches and camps we weren't home much anyway. In July we were advised we would be working at our Missionary Training Institute near Fredonia, Wisconsin. We moved from Michigan to Wisconsin before the fall term began.

This Institute, which is about forty miles north of Milwaukee is one of six such schools operated by our New Tribes Mission in the United States and Canada. From the beginning they were dubbed "boot camps" because of the rather rugged training given. These Institutes, or camps, are always located in the country. Living accommodations are supposed to somewhat approximate those of the mission field. Single people live in dormitories and are required to do their own cooking. Married couples and families have small apartments that provided only the essentials. When we took our boot camp training in 1949 we lived in a small cabin with no refrigerator, running water, or inside plumbing. Today, health code requires that most of these things be supplied. Students are not allowed to take employment during the Missions Institute training, but are encouraged to look to the Lord for the supply of their needs as they shall some day have to do in a foreign country. Of course, some may have savings from which they can draw and which they may share with others if they are led of the Lord to do so.

Mornings are given over to classes and chapel service. The classes deal with such things as the examination of a particular tribal culture. There are discussions as to how an American would go about communicating the gospel to a people of different language and culture. This was to be one of the courses Myron was to teach. Another course presents New Testament church principles. We learn how a New Testament church might be established and how it should function. Time is also spent each morning in reading letters from missionaries. Research into the environment and needs of the people with whom missionaries work is brought before the group. Students then pray for the missionaries and the people to whom they minister. These sessions are referred to as "Hold The Ropes." The mornings conclude with a chapel service in which all are free to share things learned or experienced.

Students participate each weekday afternoon in an assigned work schedule. Men might be occupied with building construction, gardening or auto and machinery repair. Ladies might be assigned to cleaning, painting or secretarial work. The point of the work schedule is not so much the accomplishment of a task, although that is important, but to reveal the attitude with which one can work under leadership and with their fellow students. If one cannot work happily and harmoniously with a team in the United States under these circumstances, he is not likely to be able to do so under the more trying circumstances of a foreign field.

Evening hours are used for study or for practical Christian work such as witnessing, Bible study, youth clubs, etc.

For six weeks in the summer all students and several staff members go to "jungle camp". This is a still more isolated location where students are required to build a house, complete with simple furnishings, from a material found in the woods. They may use canvas or plastic where waterproofing is necessary. Such skills as chopping firewood, making a cookstove from clay and metal, butchering an animal, and baking bread are required of the men. Among other things, women must learn to kill and dress a chicken. Hair cutting is also taught, especially to the wives. There are no barbers in the outlying jungle areas. Overnight hikes, canoeing and simulated survival in a jungle are also a part of the training.

In February of our furlough year, I underwent surgery in a hospital in Sheboygan, Wisconsin. The surgeon agreed with my Bolivian doctor that I indeed had been born without a gall bladder. He also spoke highly of the doctor's work. It was very convenient that Myron had an uncle and aunt living in Sheboygan where he was able to spend a night or two while

I was in the hospital. This aunt and uncle were soon to celebrate their seventy-fifth wedding anniversary at the time Myron was there.

I suppose that our furlough in 1965-66 could be thought of as the furlough of romance and marriages--at least as far as our immediate family was concerned. Ruth and Dave announced their engagement soon after our arrival in the states. Paul and Marilyn soon followed. But they were not the only ones the "love bug" had badly bitten. While we were serving in Fredonia, we entertained for dinner some missionaries from Thailand. Glen and Opal Snure and their family came and had dinner with us. They had a lovely daughter, Grace, who was about David's age. I seated David directly across the table from her and with David it was a case of love at first sight. Shortly thereafter, he was convinced that this young lady would be his future wife and told her so. I'm told her response was, "You're crazy!" or something to that effect. Crazy or not, they are married today with a lovely family. If Priscilla, our youngest had any infatuations during our furlough, we didn't hear about them.

Myron also had some physical difficulties during the year of furlough and spent the Easter weekend and several days following in the Port Washington hospital because of a staph infection. Several other events also highlighted our furlough in Wisconsin.

Each year our Mission has several conferences throughout the United States and in Canada. But in 1966 there was only one annual conference. It was held at Camp Awana, which is not too far from Fredonia where we lived. During one weekend of the conference there were six hundred people present including eighty of our missionaries from various countries of the world. It was a week of joyous reunion with many with whom we had become acquainted through the years, and a time of spiritual blessings and challenge as well. Another highlight of that spring, was Ruth's graduation from the Grand Rapids School of Bible and Music. Scholastically, she graduated second highest in a class of fifty-one students. This accomplishment was reached only by diligence and the grace of God, since she also carried on employment to meet her expenses.

During this same year, I was also studying and making preparations to become a United States citizen. A few weeks later while we were in Michigan helping to prepare for Ruth's wedding, I received word from the immigration office in Milwaukee that I must appear for a hearing relative to my becoming a citizen of the United States on the day before Ruth's wedding. This year had been the first opportunity I had to become an American. Formerly it was required of one to live 5 years at one address. We never had more than one year at a time in the States. This meant that I had to travel to Milwaukee and back that same day, meet friends in Milwaukee who were to be my witnesses, and take a difficult test in American history, etc. all of this happened the day before the big occasion. To delay was not appropriate because in July we were to return to Bolivia. As usual, everything worked out fine, although it was rather a hectic and difficult day for all of us.

Just two weeks after Ruth and Dave were married, the knot was tied for Paul and Marilyn. Some rather tense moments preceded that occasion too. For one thing, Paul failed to secure the marriage license sufficiently in advance--I suppose being a "missionary kid" he didn't know about such things. There would not have been a wedding as planned had not Pat Zondervan interceded for him before the local official. In addition, David's suitcase did not arrive with him on the bus from Milwaukee so, as best man at the wedding, he wore one of Myron's suits with the pants considerably gathered in at the waist.

During these busy weeks of weddings and meetings we were so grateful to Edna Richardson of Clarksville, Michigan, who made her home open to us while we were in the area.

The time passed quickly and we were soon saying sad "goodbyes" to Paul and Marilyn and Dave and Ruth. Once again we headed for Florida, and Boliva. Our son, David drove us to Forida, because he was buying our car and would drive it back to Waukesha, Wisconsin, where both he and his friend Grace were enrolling at the New Tribes Bible Institute.

As we left Michigan, we were once again to experience God's faithfulness. Most missionaries do not mention financial needs unless they are asked. Before leaving Clarksville we were asked if we had sufficient money for our fares. To this Myron responded, "Yes." We were not asked if we had enough money for our large amount of excess baggage. Myron didn't tell anyone we lacked for that. The Lord allowed our faith to be tested until we reached his sister's home in Florida. We received a phone call from the pastor of the Bible Church there. The message was that another missionary had deposited two hundred dollars to our account and that the church was adding another one hundred dollars. This word reached us just the day before we needed to confirm our plane reservations. It was more than adequate to make up that which we lacked! What man would think of as an impossibility, proved to us once again that we serve the God of miracles.

At 8 o'clock on a hot, humid evening in July 1966 we said goodbye to David and Myron's sister Frances and boarded a Peruvian airliner at Miami's International Airport. It was apparent that we were headed for South America because of the many Latins on board. At about midnight we landed at Panama where everyone was required to disembark for thirty minutes. Again it was hot and humid. As 6:30 a.m. we arrived in Lima, Peru only to learn that the Bolivian Airline on which we were scheduled to fly had cancelled it's flight to La Paz and Cochabamba. Since we had booked our flights all the way through to Cochabamba, Myron refused to pass Peruvian customs until we were assured that our accommodations in Lima and subsequent flight to Cochabamba were going to be taken care of properly. Because he held firmly to his conviction that the "hitch" in our travel plans was the airline's fault and not ours, we were put in a fine hotel at the airline's expense. Later, for an additional seventy-five dollars, we were given reservations on a United States' Airline with departure scheduled early the next morning. What baggage we did not need at the hotel was to be locked in a storeroom at the airport until the next morning.

Myron picks up the story. "At six thirty in the morning, Joy, Priscilla and I arrived at the airport and I set about finding someone who would release our stored baggage as I had been promised. However, there was no one at the Peruvian airlines counter so I telephoned a number I had been given the day before. I received only a sleepy response at the other end of the line. Eventually the owner of the voice appeared. Then he couldn't find a key to the store room and he asked me to help him look. Here I was, a passenger behind the counter going through all kinds of drawers trying to find a key. In the meantime, the time for our flight was drawing closer and closer. We still didn't even have our baggage in hand. Not finding a key, we went to the door of the storeroom where the man I had phoned pounded on the door until the guard inside awoke and opened it.

Our baggage was supposed to have been securely locked within a "cage" inside the storeroom. Instead, one suitcase was missing and only the front cover of our large shortwave radio (a gift from a faithful supporter) was with our baggage. I began to look around. The radio stood on the guard's desk where he had enjoyed playing it throughout the night and one suitcase stood on some building materials in one corner of the room probably to be carried off by someone at an opportune time. With the Lord's help, I 'kept my cool', gathered my things together and headed for the United States Airline's counter."

"By this time all the passengers had their luggage weighed and the plane was about to depart. Joy, Priscilla and I had been praying that the Lord would help us recover our baggage and get us on the plane and he did! We would have been left behind had it not been for an employee of the airline, an American, who saw our predicament, and said to the girl at the counter, "Don't bother weighing their baggage; accept the figure that was arrived at in Miami." She agreed and we boarded the plane enjoying the same discount in excess baggage weight that had been extended us by the Peruvian airline.

It was great to be on that plane and enjoy a lovely breakfast of eggs and sausage as we flew over the Andes Mountains to La Paz. I guess this revitalized us for the changing of planes and the passing of Bolivian customs in La Paz. It is not uncommon for a newcomer to faint from the high altitude and lack of oxygen. We had to do a little talking to get our things passed without duty but managed to do so as we explained to the official that we were not tourists but missionaries who worked for the well-being of their people and country.

Late that afternoon we were at our mission headquarters in Cochabamba. We were met at the airport by our field chairman and his wife. From hot, humid, Miami we had come to cold, dry Cochabamba in the Andes Mountains. Outwardly we were shivering, but we were warm on the inside because we were among friends!

Picking Up The Threads

◆◆◆

Chapter 16

Once back in Bolivia, it had to be decided by the Field Committee, of which Myron was a member, just where we were most needed on the field. Would it be headquarters there in Cochabamba? It was decided we were needed most at Tambo. Myron became Vice-Director of the school. That is if the director suddenly collapsed or was away, Myron would be in command of the school. He was also the business manager which included being the bookkeeper. He would also teach bookkeeping and ninth and tenth grade English. Together we would supervise the high school girls dorm. In addition, I would serve as school nurse and train some of our national hired workers to do the school laundry.

Our home was set up in two rooms of the dorm. This dorm was the newest building on the campus. In fact, it was still unfinished. There was as yet no plumbing, no ceilings and no glass in the windows. Since it was located on the windward side of our school's soccer field, which had only recently been leveled by a bulldozer, every breeze brought dust and dirt into the dormitory. Myron countered some of the unpleasantness by tacking plastic over our windows but because there was still an open space under the eaves the wind continued to carry dirt up under the eaves and deposit it on top of our beds and furniture. It was not only dusty and dirty, it was also cold. Because of the altitude of nearly five thousand feet, and the early spring of the year, the temperature sometimes went down to as low as forty degrees. It was not uncommon for staff and students to be seen bundled up in their heaviest sweaters, and even top coats.

Chapter 16

Unlike older buildings on campus, our dormitory was not built of adobe blocks which are made of mud, grass and water, but of blocks made of dampened soil and a small amount of cement. This mixture was compressed by a simple hand-operated machine into blocks about half the size of our cement blocks in the United States. I understand that this technique was devised with the intention of providing underdeveloped nations with a low cost building material. In our experience, it has proven quite satisfactory providing the blocks are laid upon a substantial concrete foundation. Even then, these blocks have not proven as resistant to earthquakes as are the age-old adobe blocks held together by dry grass.

As the new school year began late in August, we welcomed a new cook and his wife. A new single teacher also joined the team, as a teacher for some of the lower grades. At the same time we had the unpleasant experience of dismissing a teacher from the Mission altogether, and putting another missionary on probation. Such disciplinary action consumed hours and hours of time with the Field committee, with our meetings lasting at times until the wee hours of the morning.

I really enjoyed the ministry with the high school girls. We had devotions together each evening after their study hall. It was a joy to have the different girls share what the Lord was doing in their lives. Our hearts went up to the Lord in prayer for some who were not walking with Him, and others who had not received him as their own personal Savior.

In the midst of all this some of us still found time to share the Word of God in local assemblies. Myron and I frequently visited the village of Mataral and the leprosarium in Los Negros where we had formerly worked. We always received a warm welcome from our friends, whom we endeavored to encourage in the Lord.

August is the month of our wedding anniversary and on the appropriate date, Priscilla remembered us with a card and some home made candy. Myron said the best he could do was a gift to me of four Bolivian-made chocolate bars!

Advancements were made in the completion of our dormitory building during the first several months of our occupancy. As ceilings were put in, and walls plastered, we were required to move from room to room. After the plumbing was installed, the pump for pumping water from the river to a storage tank went bad and for several days all water, even for the bathrooms, had to be hauled in barrels with the school pickup. Before Christmas of that year we were comfortably settled, however, and the water pump was working well too. At about that time, we became the happy possessors of an apartment size bottled gas kitchen stove. Bolivia, at last, had become a producer of bottled gas and after seventeen years of cooking with wood or kerosene, we were now to enjoy the convenience of a gas stove.

For Myron, classes too were going well. In his ninth and tenth grade English class an incident occurred which Myron relates. "I had asked my students to write sentences using the words 'later' and 'latter'. After several had given me good examples of the proper use of the words, a ninth grade girl raised her hand and said, "Mr. Gess, I have something different. I have, 'The child climbed the latter.'" To this the girl's older brother, who was in the tenth grade, but in the same classroom, groaned and said, 'Oh, Nancy!'"

We found ourselves very weary most of the time however. A visiting doctor found my blood pressure very low. Because of this, all responsibilities except that of the dorm and the school clinic, were given to someone else. We continued to reach out into the surrounding villages, however, with the Word of God on Sundays. We also began morning services in the home of a believer about three miles from the school. Usually we made this trip on foot and found it a bit taxing in the heat of the day.

Myron was also asked to speak at the graduation banquet for a secondary school for Bolivians in the city of Santa Cruz. This was a Christian school and one of the graduates was a young man from the village of Mataral where the Lord has used us to establish a small church. This fine young man had not had many educational opportunities offered him in his village, yet he graduated from the school with the second highest grades. He eventually became a teacher.

At Christmas time we were invited to the village of Mataral, where the believers had prepared a very fine Christmas program. Helping in this program was an elderly man named Ricardo, who had been saved from a life of wickedness by the power of the Gospel. To Myron's surprise, he called him to the platform and pinned on the lapel of his coat a hand woven, cloth motto which read "God of Peace -- 1966" and said, "This is in recognition of Don Mario's (what he was called in Spanish) having come to teach us the message of salvation." It was in the will of God that before the week was over this old gentleman was in the presence of his Redeemer, having lost his life as he was washed down a gully by a flash flood caused by heavy rains in the mountains. He had also joined his wife who had passed away less than a year before. His body was laid to rest beside that of his wife in a tomb which he had constructed out of adobe blocks with his own hands and on his own property. The words spoken by a Bolivian pastor at the funeral, as well as story of Ricardo's life were messages of God's offer of salvation to the many of the town people who gathered. In our own heart often came the question. "What would have been the destiny of Ricardo and others had we not gone to the village?" I also ask myself, "Are some still lost somewhere because we haven't been as faithful as we should have been?" I wonder if there will be others to pick up the threads when the Lord takes us Home.

As a family that year we had only a simple Christmas celebration. Only Priscilla was with us but letters from the three other children who were in the United States, assured us that all was well with them in their respected places of training for the Lord's work. David sent us the special morsel of news that he was giving Grace a ring for Christmas, and that the Bible school staff had given them permission to marry the following June.

The Bolivians have a marriage custom which is quite different from anything in the United States. In Bolivia when one plans to marry he or she may go to a friend and say, "I would like you to be my 'padrino'." Now, the term "padrino" usually means "godfather" but it can also mean "groomsman" or patron". So a prospective bride may ask a friend to provide her gown or the wedding cake. A groom may ask a friend to buy his suit or bear the expense of the wedding pictures. It so happened that the young man who graduated from secondary school with honors, decided to get married and asked if Myron would be his "padrino" and purchase his wedding suit. Well, at that time, we had three children who were putting themselves through school with almost no financial help from us. They had also paid for most of the expenses of their own weddings. They knew their "missionary parents" weren't any wealthier than they. Because of this, we didn't respond too warmly to his request of serving as his 'Padrino'. However, not wanting to discourage this young couple, who were also entering the Lord's work, we gave him a sum of money which would help him considerably toward the purchase of a suit.

The evening of the wedding was an evening early in February and the ceremony took place in the first "evangelical" church of Mataral (literally the first and only "evangelical" church of Mataral). The church had only a mud floor and the pews were made of split cactus wood. There were flowers, however, in the form of two large house plants growing in some square 5 gallon tin cans in which lard had been purchased. These plants stood at either side of the pulpit and in one can, beside the flowers, was a stalk of corn about two feet high which no one had the heart to pull out. The bride wore a beautiful chiffon dress with veil and train and the groom was handsome in a dark blue suit. There were attendants and a ring bearer. I walked down the aisle with the bride and Myron with the groom. As I recall, the ceremony was performed by a national pastor, a friend of the groom. Following the ceremony a reception was held at the home of the groom's parents who lived a couple miles out in the country. We never received much news from the newlyweds after the wedding, but trust they lived happily ever after.

Having sold our Chevrolet carryall before going home on furlough, we had been without a vehicle of our own since our return. However, since we left the work of the leprosarium our need for transportation was not as great as it once was, but we still wished for something to get us to and from the little churches we visited from time to time.

Another member of our Mission, Mabel Hurst, had a 1949 army type Jeep for sale, since she was expecting a new one to arrive from the United States. It wasn't the most beautiful thing to look at and it rode like a tractor, but when most vehicles in Bolivia sold for several thousand, her price of five hundred dollars was rather attractive. We decided to buy it, but to transfer the ownership of a vehicle in Bolivia is not a simple matter. The transfer in this case was further complicated by the death of her husband, Norman. He had been washing this same Jeep at a nearby river when he suffered a heart attack, fell into the river and was drowned.

Since the transfer had to be done by a lawyer in the city of Santa Cruz, one hundred and twenty miles from us, Myron traveled all night by bus to reach the city, spent all of the following day making the transfer of ownership and then drove the Jeep back to our mission school yet that evening. He arrived at midnight and found me and some high school girls in the clinic delivering a baby for a Bolivian woman. You can be sure that all of us were glad when the mother was resting comfortably and we all could at last go to bed.

A maintenance man at school welded some steel sheets over the rusted-out floor boards in that eighteen year old Jeep and eventually, Priscilla and Myron brushed on a coat of dark green paint. In fact, someone said it was only the paint that kept the thing together. However, we sold the jeep to a national pastor before we left for our next furlough. About twelve years after we sold it, someone told us they saw the same Jeep still in use in the city of Cochabamba. In Bolivia, cars just do not die! One could say that automobiles are so expensive, they just aren't allowed to die.

A couple of years later our daughter and son-in-law came to Bolivia as missionaries. It took five months for them to get their Toyota jeep-type vehicle released from customs after it's entry into the country. The customs fee was two thousand, four hundred dollars, in spite of the fact that our Mission had a contract with the Bolivian government which is supposed to guarantee us freedom from duty on such large items of equipment. If you add two thousand four hundred dollars to the three thousand dollars they paid for this 1971 vehicle here in the the United States, plus shipping charges from New Orleans to Peru, you can see that your automobile becomes rather valuable by the time it reaches Bolivia. However, a new one purchased in Bolivia would have cost them nearly twenty thousand dollars.

Well, back to life at the school for missionary children. With busy days that started at about five thirty or six each morning, and didn't end until at least ten at night, another semester of school quickly passed. We found ourselves preparing for three days of graduation activities which would be followed by a week of field conferences. My big job was arranging sleeping accommodations for the many visitors. We expected about seventy guests for graduation but more than ninety arrived. Every available space was used, you can be sure.

This graduation was Priscilla's big occasion because she was graduating from high school. At the time the diplomas were awarded, Priscilla was also given the "good character" award. She was following in the steps of her older sister to whom it had been twice awarded in previous years.

With the arrival of the long vacation there also came not only an exodus of students, but also an exodus of many staff members. Some went to visit relatives in other countries of South America. Others left the school to help in other areas of the work. Still others began their year of furlough. Those of us who remained were not idle because there was still a fair amount of office work to be done and an even larger amount of summer maintenance. Some of us not-so-mechanically-minded were really challenged when a diesel generator or some other piece of equipment failed to function.

THE "JAM" DEAL

A vacation time at the school is always characterized by its irregularities but there was one particular irregularity in the summer of 1967 that really threw remaining staff members for a loop. Unknown to Myron, who was business manager at the school, another staff member had ordered eight hundred quarts or four fifty gallon barrels of jam from a Mennonite colony in the lowlands of Bolivia. Now, there was nothing wrong with the jam which was made from a flowering fruit called "grosella" it was the quantity and the cost of two hundred and seventy-five dollars which the school could ill afford at that time. What do you do with four barrels of jam that arrives in unsealed containers in a tropical climate? To begin with, you find every large kettle on the property and boil the jam until it is again sterile and then try to find enough containers into which you can somehow seal the sweet, sticky, perishable substance. This is an experience about which we could all laugh later on, but at the time it was not at all funny! To top it off, our Mission buyer in the city of Santa Cruz, who was a good friend of the Mennonites, sent a radio message requesting that we send more containers for more jam. I think at that point, Myron's response was, "only over my dead body!"

A sadder incident of that vacation period was the death of our gardener's little girl. Our gardener was a Quechua Indian by the name of Antonio who lived across the road from the school. He had professed to have received the Lord as his Saviour, but had a terrible problem with drink. A few months previously, Myron had been called to his home by his wife because he had come home drunk after having spent all his wages, including vacation pay. He had mistreated her and had torn up her clothing. Now his little girl had died and we buried her in the little cemetery on our property. Antonio was too drunk and too embarrassed to attend the service.

On June tenth of that year, David and Grace were married in Waukesha, Wisconsin. Myron had to send a notarized permission because David was not yet twenty-one. Although the wedding was lovely, the only relatives in attendance from our side of the family were Paul and Ruth. Some dear friends from Clarksville, Michigan, drove all the way to Waukesha, however, for the occasion. This was just one of the many instances when friends in Michigan, in Christian love, sort of substituted for us while we were far away. In order that we might celebrate the occasion too, Myron, Priscilla and I drove to the village of Comarapa, where we had a delicious meal in a so-called hotel for the price of sixty cents each. At that time, food costs were low in Bolivia.

A Sad Farewell

Chapter 17

With many staff members away from the school during vacation, we who remained were kept very busy with an assortment of duties. This made the weeks pass quickly and before we knew it, the middle of August had arrived and that meant it was time for Priscilla, our youngest and last, to leave for the United States. Shortly before she was to leave, I had a birthday dinner in her honor and prepared one of Priscilla's favorite meals, roast chicken and dressing. The chicken was not the almost tasteless supermarket variety we get here in the United States, but a truly "homegrown" chicken, rich in flavor.

We wanted so much to take Priscilla to Cochabamba in our Jeep but weren't sure that we should launch out on a more than two hundred mile trip in such an old vehicle. One reason we wanted so much to make the trip in the Jeep was that we wanted to take a side trip over a very rugged road. There were some Inca ruins which as a family we had never seen. Finally, after weighing the pros and cons, and with much prayer, we decided to risk it. The little car was much taller than it was long by the time we had our baggage, Priscilla's baggage and a spare can of gasoline tied on the top carrier. We had to carry other items for emergencies too. There were only a couple of gas stations and no garages between us and Cochabamba.

We left Tambo early in the morning and at about two-thirds of the way to Cochabamba took a side road toward the Inca ruins. The road was quite good for a short distance, but then a river became the road bed, and we had to drive in this shallow river bed for some distance over stones a foot or more high. After leaving the river, the road became so steep Myron had to put the Jeep in the lowest four-wheel drive possible. After an hour and a half of this we reached the ruins. They consisted of the walls of a large building which likely had been a temple, and the broken walls and foundations of several smaller buildings. However, the construction was only of round stones and not of the finely hewn rocks characterizing most Inca ruins. Nevertheless, we had the satisfaction of seeing them.

We made the arduous trip back to the 'highway' and proceeded on to Cochabamba. The Jeep continued to perform well, for which we were so thankful. When we reached the city one small deficiency showed up and became a major deficiency in the city. The horn wouldn't blow! Now in most areas of Cochabamba there are not stop signs or traffic lights at the intersections. One proceeds toward an intersection, blows his horn, and if he hears no other horn blow, he proceeds at normal speed through the intersection. Because the streets are narrow and have buildings on each side, one drives almost as in a tunnel until he reaches the cross street. Such driving in a properly functioning car is not for the newly arrived American or the faint at heart but to be without a horn was indeed inviting disaster. Somehow or other, however, we crossed the entire city and breathed a sigh of relief when we were safely at our Mission home. The following day a mechanic concluded that the Jeep needed not only a new horn, but a new generator as well.

We had a couple of happy final days in the city with Priscilla. One day a fellow missionary took all of us up Mount Tunari, which is often snow-covered. One can see the city of Cochabamba below. Unfortunately, we had to turn back at about seventeen thousand feet because I became quite ill from the high altitude. I often say to myself, that when the Lord comes for His own, I won't be worrying about the altitude!

There was also a lovely farewell for Priscilla at the mission home. Then arrived the rather tearful moment when we had to say good-bye and see her and a classmate board a plane for Lima, Peru and then to the United States. Oh how we trusted the Lord that He and He alone would take care of those two girls traveling alone over so many miles. This was the fourth time we had been parted from our offspring in about the same way. Does repetition make it easier? I don't think so, but it's in times like these that we experience that "all-sufficient" grace of the Lord Jesus.

Having seen Priscilla off by plane to the United States, Myron and I rather sadly reversed our bumpy ride in the little old Jeep to the mission school. Once again we made the two hundred mile trip without serious difficulty.

It was the month of August and almost time for school to reopen, but two of our staff families including our director and his wife, had not yet returned from visiting relatives in other parts of South America. In addition to this, we received word from our mission headquarters in the States that two new staff families would be delayed a month in arriving! We didn't panic, but we did have some serious thoughts as to what we would do if even our regular personnel didn't return in time. We endeavored to rest in the fact that the Lord has matters under his control even when we don't.

All of our regular staff members did return before the opening day of school, but they were tired from their travels and the uncertainties and pressures of getting things off to a start were felt by all of us. Missionaries, you know, are not super human or super-spiritual people but ordinary people through whom God sometimes chooses to perform extraordinary tasks. Consequently, some misunderstandings and feelings arose on that opening day of school about who was to do what. We were thankful that almost as quickly as they arose, we were able to resolve them in the Lord.

Because our teacher for the seventh and eighth grades was not arriving for a month, it had to be decided who could substitute for her. It seemed best that we handle these two grades, as we would the high school. Several teachers would take two grades with each teacher taking certain subjects. One of these teachers would also be in charge of the classroom. It was concluded that Myron would teach Bible, spelling, English and Spanish and be in charge of the classroom. He would also continue teaching English I and bookkeeping in high school. He was to do the school bookkeeping, keeping his eye on the school finances. After regular school hours he would be a dorm "father". I would carry the major load of supervising the high school girls' dorm, serve as nurse for the school and community. I was also school hostess. I would also try to fit twenty or more piano pupils for private lessons, into my schedule. It's a good thing we were a little younger then.

As with any vacation, there were always those unplanned incidents that embellished the regular schedule. For example, on the evening of the "Get acquainted" party held during the first week of school, one of the older high school boys kept one of our new high school girls out much later than school rules allowed since we staff members felt keenly our responsibility to guard carefully the moral and spiritual well-being of the students placed in our care, both Myron and the director of the school had to deal rather severely with the offending boy.

Also, because Myron was a member of the Field Committee, or governing body of the field, there occasionally arose matters that had to be cared for. One such situation arose shortly after the opening of school. One of our single lady missionaries, who was not well, labored in a remotely located area and we were concerned about her welfare. Our field chairman, whose home was in Cochabamba, first traveled to our school and then he, along with our school chairman and Myron, started off in the school's pickup Sunday morning enroute to this missionary's home. Along the way, they stopped at the leprosarium and invited our missionary dentist, Paul Mason, to accompany them. It was an arduous four and one half hour trip over sandy roads. Somewhere along the way the truck sputtered and stopped. Apparently they had a clogged up fuel line but even after blowing the line out with the tire pump, nothing would work until the fuel tanks were changed. They didn't reach their destination until after two p.m. They found our missionary friend about to begin a Bible study with some Bolivian neighbors, so they joined the group. Later, she served our men some cake, canned peaches and Kool-aid which they really appreciated. The men hadn't eaten since they left Tambo. On the way home they stopped at a former leprosy patient's home and were served "empanadas". They never reached home until eleven o'clock that night, so their Sunday was not an especially restful one. Our lady missionary was grateful for their visit and the men had a great day of fellowship in the Lord.

Sharing from Myron's journal: "We have shared with you that we were seriously understaffed as we began the fall 1967 semester at the school for missionary children. Consequently, we often were very weary but didn't know where we could cut back on our activities. It appears that one Sunday evening the Lord ordered a rest for us. Joy and I, together with some high school students started off in our little old Jeep for the village of Mataral to help in the meeting there. We went a few miles when I noticed that the generator didn't seem to be charging. We returned to the school where our mechanic thought it was only the voltage control sticking. He supposedly corrected this and we started off again. This time, as we passed through a village about a mile from the school a boy threw a stone at the Jeep which completely shattered a side window. Fortunately no one was injured by the flying glass. We continued, our trip but after several miles the lights blinked so badly, we returned once again to the school. I couldn't understand why we had not been allowed to make the trip until I opened my Bible and read, "The steps of a good man are ordered by the Lord; and he delighteth in his way." Ps. 37:23 I think the Lord knew we needed a rest! Incidentally, later our school mechanic found a defective bearing in the generator, a bearing which was supposed to have been replaced by a mechanic in Cochabamba and for which I had paid a good fee."

Both Myron and I had our frequent times of illness at the school. One week was especially hard because, in addition to my not being well myself. I had ten students in bed with one kind of illness or another. Besides this there were seventeen visitors to the school who required sleeping accommodations.

We were glad that fall to eventually welcome two newcomers to the staff -- Merlin and Marion Schultz. Merlin was to be our new cook and Marion was to help in various ways. It's interesting that when our daughter Ruth attended the Grand Rapids School of Bible and Music, Marion was her floor supervisor and showed her, as a newcomer to the States, many favors. Ruth and Paul in turn challenged her about needs in Bolivia. The result was she took our missions training course, met her husband there, and came to Bolivia as a missionary.

In the meantime, we were receiving letters from Priscilla telling us how various ones in the Clarksville area had befriended her. She had also secured part time employment as a clerk at Woolworth's while attending Bible School. We were soon to hear about her first date, as well.

Occasionally at the school for missionary children a "Going Home" weekend is scheduled for students whose homes are close enough for them to go there. On this particular weekend so many had gone that we had only seven girls in our dorm. Since there were so few, on Saturday evening we decided that we would take all of them in our Jeep to the "hotel" in a nearby village for supper. We also had with us the two small children of a staff couple who had to go to Cochabamba for medical reasons. You should have seen the looks when Myron stopped the jeep in front of the hotel, opened the back door and allowed no less than eleven people to spill out! I don't know if we had set a record or not!

Another special occasion of the semester was Field Day, which really consisted of several days of athletic activities with many parents attending. For this particular Field Day there were forty-five guests. It started with a challenging cross-country race by high school boys before classes began on Thursday morning. There was nothing more until Friday when the entire day and Saturday morning, as well, were given over to athletic competitions. The activities might have extended into Saturday afternoon had not so many students required bandaged hands from a "wheelbarrow" race held on gravelly soil. Unfortunately for him, Myron was so far behind in his work that he used the time of Field Day doing bookkeeping.

Then there was a Spiritual Emphasis weekend. A couple from another mission came as our special speakers. The Lord's ministry through them was effective in our own hearts as well. He showed us that we should endeavor to be content and faithful in our work at the school, although the way was difficult.

I am sure you realize that children of missionaries sometimes have problems as other children have. When these problems arose at our school for missionary children and became serious, we asked for a conference with the child's parents. In the fall semester of 1967 we met with the parents of one of our high school girls. The girl had two evident problems. One, she really didn't want to be at Tambo. Secondly, she was (or thought she was) in love with a Bolivian bus driver who drove the route between Cochabamba and Santa Cruz. He made frequent stops at Tambo either to receive or let off passengers. How this girl came to know this bus driver, I'm not sure. It could have been while she was on vacation in Cochabamba, or as a passenger on the bus. At any rate, she was infatuated with him and made it clear to her parents that she hoped someday to marry him. Nothing that her parents told her concerning racial or cultural differences could dissuade her in her thinking.

We, as dorm parents, had to keep a very close rein on her, because she sought every possible opportunity to communicate with this man. We did a lot of praying about this matter. We as her dorm supervisors had a meeting with her and her parents. The ultimatum was given that she change her attitude and behavior, or else leave the school. She professed a change of heart and things went better from then on. She never married the bus driver, but rather a few years later, when we were on staff at our Bible School in Waukesha, Wisconsin, she came to the school as a student. The Lord used us once again to counsel and comfort her during another love affair which didn't consummate in marriage either. The story does have a happy ending. The young lady went out as a single missionary to Venezuela. There she met a fine young man of another mission who chose her as his bride. Just after their marriage Myron and I were visiting in Bolivia for several weeks, and met them on their honeymoon. They seemed so ideally suited to one another and although we were tempted, we didn't ask the young lady if she was sorry she never married the Bolivian bus driver. Her parents thanked us for having dealt with her firmly during her difficult teenage years.

Because Myron continued to have many digestive problems during those months, we asked the staff for permission to cook and eat our meals in our own dormitory. This required considerable deliberation because everyone knew that if some staff members were allowed to do it, others would want to do it too just to escape the common dining hall atmosphere. Eventually, we were granted the privilege. Now we are told, many other staff members enjoy the same privilege.

After school closed for the Christmas vacation that year it took several days for Myron and me to get caught up in our work. Once we had done so, we took off with light hearts for a few days rest in the city of Santa Cruz. While there, Myron consulted a doctor about his persistent health problems.

Returning to Tambo, we had a lovely Christmas dinner at our dorm with all staff present. It wasn't a complete Christmas for us, however, because it was the first Christmas we were bereft of all our children. The chairman of the school remarked later that he never saw a more dejected looking person in all his life than Myron was while sitting alone on the front steps of our dorm on Christmas afternoon.

It wasn't long after that however, that we had much cause for rejoicing. We received word from Paul and Marilyn that they hoped to be on their way to Bolivia as missionaries the following summer and would help us celebrate our twenty-fifth wedding anniversary in the month of August.

With the beginning of the second semester I took on the additional responsibility of teaching a high school typing class four nights a week. Both of our schedules were full to the limit.

The months of November through February, generally speaking, are the hottest, wettest months of the year in Bolivia. Consequently there are often landslides in the mountains. At the time of a "Going Home weekend," we had the unfortunate experience of having a landslide blocking the highway on either side of Tambo. For several days, both our mail and supplies were cut off. What was even worse, two of our girl students were marooned for a day, a night and another day on a bus blocked by the landslide between our school and they city of Santa Cruz. They were eventually "rescued" by our mission buyer and suffered no ill effects from their experience.

NEW RECRUITS FOR BOLIVIA

In our Mission's training course one goes to language school after he has finished Missionary Training Institute. Upon entering language school, he is given tests to determine whether he is a slow, average or fast learner and if he or she might have special abilities in the analysis and breakdown of new languages. It is interesting that both our daughter Ruth and daughter-in-law Marilyn were discovered to be possessors of special linguistic ability. As a result near the completion of their language school training they were asked to leave their husbands for six weeks while they lived and studied with a tribe of American Indians near the Wisconsin Dells. Although they saw their husbands on occasion, neither they nor their husbands were very happy about this period of separation.

At about the time they were completing their course of training in Wisconsin, we were winding up another semester of school at Tambo. One day a photographer from Cochambamba came to take pictures for the year book. He set up his equipment in the chapel and as each member posed for his picture there were several others standing around making comments and helping the one being photographed to smile. In addition, one of our lady staff members, Mabel Hurst, who plays the piano by ear, sat at the piano and played what she thought was an appropriate song while each of us posed for the photographer. We laughed when she played "Silver Threads Among the Gold" for me, but we really roared when for her eighty-two year old mother, known to all as "Mom" Janofski, she played, "The Old Gray Mare, She Ain't What She Used to Be!" Both mother and daughter had a great sense of humor and everyone knew that no disrespect whatever was being shown. This dear old mother lived another nine years at Tambo, and in her more feeble years was lovingly cared for by her daughter Mable. She went to be with the Lord whom she loved while there in Tambo and is buried in our little Tambo cemetery.

Graduation activities early in May went well with the intermediate grades putting on a play entitled, "The Life Of Hudson Taylor." This was enjoyed by everyone. I had the responsibility for the piano students' concert and the reception following graduation. The members of the Field Committee of which Myron was one met during every spare moment of graduation and field conference. The day beginning before six and almost never ended before eleven at night.

Several high school boys stayed on after graduation to help demolish the old school kitchen so that a new one could be built. They took their meals with us during that time. There was also always the medical work I was responsible for even though it was vacation time. Neighbors in the surrounding area would come seeking help for their physical needs. I delivered a baby boy for a Bolivian neighbor whose husband had died with a heart attack just a few weeks earlier. This had left her a widow and the mother of eight children. We were glad she was a Christian, because obviously her future wasn't going to be an easy one.

After the work was sufficiently caught up for us to leave, Myron and I traveled to the city of Santa Cruz on one of Bolivia's newer buses. It was comfortable but the driver was terrible. He blew his horn and took the inside of every blind curve at full speed. All we could do was call upon the Lord for protection. As we rounded one curve we came upon a road repair truck parked directly in the middle of the highway. In some miraculous way the driver stopped just before hitting the truck. We were truly thankful when that trip was over!

Dave Lotz, the Chairman of the school, and Myron had some interesting times that vacation period trying to keep the water pump motor and light generators running since neither of them were mechanics. In spite of the time spent on these things and the regular office work, Myron was able to build some cupboards for our dormitory kitchen and a cabinet for his office.

On July 18 Paul and Marilyn arrived in Cochabamba as missionaries for the field. You can be sure we were on hand to meet them. What a joy it was to see them and also to meet our little grandson Tim, whom we were seeing for the first time. Safely packed among diapers and other soft material was a beautiful cuckoo clock which they had brought as a gift from all our children for our twenty-fifth wedding anniversary. Myron remarked that future life promised to be a quiet one - fourteen high school girls and a cuckoo clock.

Paul's first job as a missionary was to be buyer for the field with he and his family living in Cochabamba. It is interesting that this had also been Myron's first responsibility as a missionary nineteen years earlier. The only difference was that at that time there were less missionaries to be served so Myron was both buyer and bookkeeper and sometimes government representative.

It was nice having Paul as a Mission buyer in Cochabamba because that meant that we could hear his voice twice each day as he communicated by radio with other missionaries throughout the field. Since Myron was the radio operator much of the time for Tambo, this also meant that Paul and his Dad could personally exchange a few words. They had to be few because of the short time allotted to each of our stations. One day their conversation brought forth a chuckle from everyone listening even though they were conducting Mission business. Myron was in need of money for the school's expenses so he said to Paul, "Paul would you send me ten thousand Bolivianos for the school account?" His answer was, "Of course I'll send you some money, Dad; you always gave me money whenever I asked for it!"

There were just three weeks left before the fall semester was to begin and the new kitchen was still without a roof; neither had the two new kerosene stoves arrived. We could have panicked but we didn't. We remembered that conditions never seemed to be perfect for the opening of school and we always managed somehow.

Dangerous Roads - God's Protection

Chapter 18

We were eating breakfast one morning when Paul and Beulah Mason, our former co-workers at the leprosarium, drove up to our dorm. Paul thought he may have had a heart attack and wondered if Myron would drive them to Cochabamba where he could see a doctor. Of course, he would, and since there was lots of room in the Volkswagon bus; I would go along too.

Things went well with us on the trip, although Myron often forgot to shift the low-powered VW to a low gear soon enough on the steep grades. At about the half-way point of the trip, however, a cloud of dust ahead on a curve in the road caught our attention. Before us we saw an open truck with passengers in the back, roll down a precipice. A little girl was killed, her mother injured and a sixteen year old girl received a badly mangled leg. Fortunately, missionaries of another mission were close behind us and were able to take the injured to Cochabamba. The highways in the mountains of Bolivia are dotted with wooden crosses where many have similarly met death.

Paul's condition was diagnosed by a doctor as not serious. Nevertheless, he and his wife stayed on in Cochabamba for a rest. Myron and I, after a delightful visit with our Paul and Marilyn and little Timmy, returned to Tambo by bus. In the course of this trip our driver, going speedily around the curves as usual, suddenly came upon a man and a woman on a motorcycle. They were taking the middle of the road to avoid potholes elsewhere. Our driver, instead of sounding his horn as soon as he saw them, waited until he was right behind them before he blasted away. This so startled the cyclist that he lost control of his cycle, swerved in front of the bus, and only by our driver taking the ditch himself, did he avoid killing them. God's guardian angels must be watching over missionaries, because in all of our Mission's thirty some years in Bolivia, we have not lost a life in travel by bus or truck!

The roof was on the new kitchen, but the new stoves had not yet arrived when school started on August twenty sixth. However, the cooks seemed to manage somehow because there was food for everyone. Several new staff members, including new teachers, were on hand, so we were looking forward to lightened schedules. None of us knew that changes far greater than that awaited us in the next semester.

By September fifteenth, Myron and twenty other students or staff were sick in bed, most of them sick with infectious hepatitis. We concluded that someone had come back from vacation already sick with the disease and had contaminated the whole school. Of course such a disease meant isolation, special diets, and all kinds of special things that created a staggering load of work for me as school nurse, and those who were recruited to help me.

Those who were well tried to look after the classes of those who were sick. After two weeks in bed, Myron was able to do his office work but was not able to teach. By October, nine of our staff members, including Dave Lotz, our director, were down with the disease. There were not enough well people left to carry on he classes and other work. We were forced to close the school. Most students returned to their homes but several were too sick to travel.

Most staff members were living in their own quarters, except the very sick who continued on in our dorm. This had been converted into a makeshift clinic where they could be cared for. Eventually, health returned to all, and everyone was on his own. Myron and I traveled to Cochabamba where I was able to get some much needed rest. Myron was to participate in Field Committee meetings.

We had a pleasant Thanksgiving Day in the year 1968 with Paul, Marilyn and little Timmy with us for that day and a day or two following. Normally, we weren't able to make Thanksgiving a very special day because this holiday is not observed in Bolivia. Life goes on as usual. Because school had been closed, however, we were free to celebrate the day as in the States. One of the desserts I was able to serve while Paul and Marilyn were with us was strawberry shortcake, made with strawberries picked from our own backyard patch. A couple of years previously, Myron had learned that strawberries were grown in some areas of Bolivia, so he bought some plants and planted them at Tambo. Now, several years later, we understand that some staff members still have strawberry plants.

At about this time we received word that our daughter Ruth and her husband David Sommer were applying for their passports to come to Bolivia as missionaries. David and Grace also informed us that they were the parents of a boy which made us grandparents for the second time. The baby, named Brett Kevin, had to be delivered by Caesarean section. Because of this medical expense, David and Grace had to drop out of the Boot Camp training course. David took employment making it possible to meet these financial obligations. We know that the Lord leads all family members differently. Our responsibility as parents is to keep them on our prayer list. It's thrilling to see how God works in separate lives.

It seemed that the amount of sunlight coming in the windows of our dorm living room was ideal for raising Africa violets. I had many beautiful plants but not enough space for them. Myron set to work making a couple of shelves that would criss-cross an entire double window which was a span of at least 20 feet. He had enough brackets for only one shelf. So, as one often does on the mission field, he had to improvise. He used the available brackets to support the top shelf and then from this suspended the shelf below with strands of plastic coated clothes line. The lack of supports actually enhanced the appearance of the shelves and flowers in front of the windows. When graduation time came, we moved those violet plants to our chapel and they decorated the platform during our commencement services.

One weekend several of the men, along with twelve Bolivian Christians, decided to make an evangelistic trip to three rather remotely located villages about thirty miles from the school. To get to these places they used a pickup truck, a motorbike and our Jeep. The road was sandy and hilly much of the way. One or two times it was necessary for them to ford a small river. They left early Saturday morning so that they could have most of Saturday and all day Sunday in these villages. Upon their arrival at the principal village of San Juan, they arranged for a Bolivian woman to cook food for the group. She was glad to do so because it meant a small earning for her. Each meal consisted of potatoes, rice and spaghetti there were no fresh vegetables or meat, except for Sunday dinner, when each of the group received a piece of chicken.

The meetings were held either at the local soccer field or in a Bolivian home situated on the main plaza of the town. Either Dave Lotz or Myron did most of the speaking, but it was also a great joy to hear their Bolivian brethren tell of their faith in Christ. Saturday night they all slept in sleeping bags or under blankets on the hard soccer field. Surprisingly enough, they all slept quite well. Before having the usual Bolivian breakfast of bread and black coffee, they peeled and ate a fresh pineapple they had brought with them. The comment, "The most delicious thing we had eaten!"

After the meetings in the village of San Juan on Saturday and Sunday, one of the Bolivian Christians, and Myron, and a student from Tambo returned to the village of Mataral to help in the service there. The other men had a meeting in a second village Sunday night with good results and left with an offer from a man there to give land for the building of a house to any missionary who would come there to live. As far as we know now, no one has yet accepted the offer. This is quite a contrast to our American towns that often have several Bible preaching churches, is it not?

Recollections

Chapter 19

Some of the things I'm writing about are being written in order that you might, in essence, enter into some of our experiences as missionaries, often separated from our children.

In the fall and winter of 1963 Priscilla wrote us from Bible school in Grand Rapids that she had been dating a young man, but that she had difficulty in knowing just how serious she should allow the relationship to become. She wasn't sure that he was the one for her. Oh, how we prayed for Priscilla. How she needed the Lord to guide her in her relationship. While we were corresponding back and forth with her we were seeking to guide her in the decisions and walk with the Lord. We were also hearing that Dave and Ruth were due to arrive in Bolivia about the middle of February. Eventually they sent us more exact information which included the name of the airline on which they were traveling and the date of their arrival. In the same letter they wrote us that Priscilla was still having doubts about her relationship with this other student in school. How much, as parents, we wished we could be with her at a time like this! We hadn't even met her friend and could hardly give her our opinion of him.

Fellow workers at Tambo kindly assumed our responsibilities for a time so that we could go to Cochabamba to meet Dave and Ruth. Paul and Marilyn, Myron and I excitedly awaited the first glimpse of Dave and Ruth at the airport, but unbelievably, they never disembarked from the plane. In fact, they weren't even on the passenger list. What could have happened? Communication between some South American countries was extremely poor in those days, but we decided we would try to learn more of their whereabouts. We did learn through a fellow missionary in Bogota, Colombia, that they had arrived there but at the last minute had cancelled their flight to Bolivia. More we could not learn. Over a period of one week we made ten trips to the Cochabamba airport to meet planes on which they might be passengers. At last they arrived, happy and healthy with the explanation that at Bogota they had been turned back at immigration because of some technicality in their papers. Dave and Ruth didn't have a lot more information about Priscilla's problems. The Lord was good, however, in allowing us to have a radio-telephone conversation with Priscilla while we were in Cochabamba. She had broken her relationship with this fellow and was at peace. We could only conclude that it was good for her to have arrived at this decision while she was still able to make it.

What about our plans for furlough? We decided that we should proceed with them in order that we might be with Priscilla during this traumatic experience.

In the meantime, Dave and Ruth accompanied us to Tambo by bus and there for several weeks helped fill a gap that was made because of lack of personnel. Although new in Bolivia, they were being effective in many areas of the work while at the same time they were studying the Spanish language.

All supplies for the school arrived at Tambo by truck from either Santa Cruz or Cochabamba. After one such arrival, growing mash for chickens was mistakenly placed in the school pantry. The following morning the Bolivian maids mistook it for cereal and cooked some of it for breakfast. Before any staff member detected the mistake some hungry youngsters had eaten it and the high school boys left the dining room crowing like roosters. Our M.K's grew fast enough without feeding them growing mash.

April 1969

We received word while still working at the school for missionary children that our son Paul and his wife Marilyn would be transferring from their work at headquarters in Cochabamba to a tribal village near the Brazilian border. They were happy about the thought of working with this new semi-civilized tribe, who in their ignorance had killed five of our missionaries in 1942.

Ruth and Dave were leaving also for the northern lowlands of Bolivia, where they were to study the Esse Ejja language with the hope of ministering to this largely unreached tribe. Myron and I traveled to Cochabamba to see them off by plane and to get our smallpox shots which we would need before we could travel to the United States.

Returning to Tambo, we went about our usual schedule of dorm supervision, nursing, teaching, making up report cards and book-keeping. At the same time we were gradually packing away some of our possessions, preparatory to a year's furlough. In addition there was another graduation to be prepared for before we left.

About the middle of June, following graduation, we had our annual field conference. Paul and Marilyn and Dave and Ruth came from their places of service for this. It was our first year to have our children attend a conference with us as full-fledged missionaries. They were also frequent contributors to the musical program during the conference. I know it was only the Lord who gave us the physical strength for the conference. In addition to the regular sessions, the members of the Field Committee had meetings each night until at least midnight. The next day began with an early morning prayer meeting. This was the pattern of each day throughout that time. In spite of tired bodies, the conference proved to be a tremendous blessing and encouragement.

With the conference over, twenty-five of us, including Dave and Ruth, traveled by bus to Cochabamba while Paul and Marilyn went in the opposite direction to their home with the Ayore Indians in Tobite. As Myron and I anticipated our trip to the United States, we remembered on July 2 that we had completed twenty years of service in Bolivia. It was on July 2, 1949 that we had first arrived. Our hearts were full of praise and gratitude to the Lord for strength and encouragement in times of trial and we anticipated additional years to serve him.

After saying good-bye to Dave and Ruth and other friends, we left Cochabamba for Peru, Panama, and the United States. Traveling with us was one of our mission representatives who had ministered at our field conference and one of our high school graduates who was returning to the United States for further study. Inasmuch as we had a four to twelve p.m. layover in Lima, Peru, we were given dinner at a fine hotel at the airline's expense and spent the evening sight-seeing. We were impressed by the many shops that offered beautifully made fur rugs. Several must have measured 8 x 10 feet in size. As they hung on the shop walls, we saw murals depicting village and mountain scenes with each object and detail made of pieces of llama fur. These were all hand-sewn. How we would have loved to purchase one, but knew that the four hundred dollar price was not within our budget.

At Miami we were separated from our mission representative and our student companion. We took an airport limousine to Fort Lauderdale where Myron's sister made her home. After a joyous reunion with her, we set about looking for a used car we could drive to Michigan and use during our furlough. Once again the Lord showed His faithfulness in leading us to a '63 Oldsmobile. We began our trip traveling north accompanied by our sister Frances. As soon as we could, we drove to South Bend, Indiana near where Priscilla was working at a children's camp for the summer. We had previously arranged a meeting place by telephone and it wasn't long before a station wagon arrived out of which bounded several girls including Priscilla. She didn't waste any time in springing into our waiting arms. Once again we knew that separations are difficult, but reunions are glorious!

One of the highlights of that furlough was the seventy-fifth anniversary celebration of the Clarksville Bible Church. Many of the former pastors and their wives participated. How good it was to fellowship with so many old friends once again and to speak of the Lord's faithfulness. Our furlough also included a trip to Canada to see friends and relatives there. We were thankful for the many opportunities the Lord gave us to tell of the work in Bolivia, and to encourage young and old to give of themselves to make the gospel known.

We shall never forget the kindness of our dear friend, Edna Richardson, who for that year of furlough, made her home our home. It was so good to be living close to Grand Rapids so that Priscilla could come home often. We could also attend the many musical programs presented by the Bible School there in Grand Rapids, Michigan.

As we enjoyed Christmas with Edna and some of our state-side relatives, we were completely unaware that at the same time our daughter Ruth in Bolivia was critically ill and in great pain. She and Dave had gone to spend Christmas with fellow-missionaries working with a very remotely located Indian tribe -- the Toromonos in north west Bolivia. While there Ruth developed an infection from an impacted wisdom tooth. The only way to get her to civilization and medical help was by air. However, it was the rainy season of the year and for several days small planes could not fly. In the meantime Ruth's jaws had locked shut and her condition became critical. Those who were aware of the situation called upon God to undertake. A missionary pilot of another mission board volunteered to attempt a flight and God opened a spot in the clouds long enough for him to land, pick up Ruth and Dave and take them to the nearest city. A medical doctor, who was one of the leading communists of the country, gave Ruth the medical aid that saved her life. From there she was flown to Cochabamba where she spent nine days in the hospital and six weeks recovering from her ordeal.

Not long after that we learned that Paul who also was in Bolivia, working with the Ayore Indians, was almost shot by one of the Indians when this man's wife had fallen off the tractor and broken her ankle. According to Ayore culture, the husband was obligated to take vengence on the one who seemed to be responsible for the injury. In this case it was Paul who was driving the tractor. Paul's life was spared. We gave glory to the Lord for once again demonstrating His faithfulness and protection.

After Priscilla's graduation she felt the Lord leading her to become a school teacher. She was accepted in Tennesse Temple Christian College in Chattanooga, Tennesse.

It was time too for us to think of purchasing tickets for our return to Bolivia. It had to be done early because those tickets were usually purchased by someone in Bolivia. We saved considerable money by doing it this way. Not only that, three young ladies from the South Boston Bible Church, who were special friends of Paul and Marilyn, wished to accompany us to Bolivia. We needed to see that their tickets were obtained as well.

These were days of many decisions and much prayer. We also needed to know the mind of the Lord as to where we should work once we were back in Bolivia. Myron had been consulting a doctor concerning his frequent stomach aches and was encouraged not to return to our mission school where the schedule was rather heavy. However, correspondence with our field leaders revealed that the need was the greatest there in Tambo. This was to replace the director of our school while he and his family took a year's furlough. Rightly or wrongly, we felt we should go where duty seemed to call.

In the meantime we had prepared seven boxes to be shipped to Bolivia by boat. One included a hospital stretcher for the school clinic which a friend had secured for us, free of charge. We were extremely grateful to several of our friends who struggled to get these boxes out of Edna's basement, banded, and on a truck by which they were taken to a freight terminal in Grand Rapids.

Following Priscilla's graduation in May, we attended our annual missionary conference at Camp Awana in Wisconsin. There Myron met with the director of our school who had already come on furlough. He needed to be brought up-to-date on things in Bolivia. We were also to learn what our responsibilities would be at Tambo for our coming year. I guess we should have known that the comparatively "light" schedule they had outlined for us was never to become a reality.

The three young ladies, Lois Bergy, Ethelyn McClure, and Grace Martin, friends of Paul and Marilyn, who were going to travel with us, were to fly from Detroit to Miami, meeting us at the Miami International Airport in time for our early morning flight to Bolivia on June 30. In the meantime, Myron and I would be driving to Miami, accompanied by Priscilla who would see us off at the airport. Before returning to Chattanooga, she would spend a few days with David and Grace who were at that time living in Florida. We said our good-byes to friends in Clarksville and headed south pulling a U-Haul trailer loaded with our baggage, and also things for Priscilla. We would leave most of her luggage with some people in Chattanooga, who were willing to store it for her until she entered college. All went well in our travels south and we had a pleasant visit with relatives in Florida before David drove us to the Miami Airport very early the morning of June 30. According to our tickets we were to fly at 9 o'clock but we arrived at the airport at 7:30 in order to have ample time to meet the three young ladies from Michigan and check our baggage together.

As we presented ourselves at the airline counter we were shocked to learn that our plane, which had been scheduled to leave at 9 a.m., had left at 4 a.m. instead. The schedule had been changed and we were never notified! The three ladies from Michigan had arrived at 1 a.m. but were ignored by the airlines employees. It was well that they were because they would have been flying to Bolivia without our companionship and help, which had been the whole point of their going with us.

Although we expressed both our dismay and displeasure, the airline employees at the airport said there was absolutely nothing they could do for us. If we wished, we could go to their office in downtown Miami and make our complaints. Fortunately David was still able to be with us and drive us downtown. The personnel at the downtown office seemed to evaluate the matter in typical "south of the border" style. "No big problem. There's always "manana" or "tomorrow!" They agreed to send us on a Pan American airline at 7 p.m. Wednesday evening. In the meantime they would put us up at a motel near the airport at their expense. They would not keep our baggage for us which meant that we had to put several pieces in lockers at the airport at $.50 a locker. The stay at the motel wasn't all that bad for Myron and me. But it was somewhat a waste of time for our three friends who were on vacation with a time limit, and had planned to spend their time in Bolivia, and not in Miami.

Well, the motel was not exactly of Holiday Inn standard. Consequently Myron and I managed to pick up some kind of "bug," probably from the food, and began to be sicker by the minute as we flew toward Bolivia. We arrived at Lima, Peru at 1:30 a.m. where we knew we needed to change planes. There was absolutely no one at the desk of the airline that had sold us our tickets. What were we to do? We surely didn't feel like sitting all night in the airport lobby with our thirty or more pieces of baggage, not even knowing when we would be leaving for our destination. A phone call to the airline's main office brought us no satisfaction but a man from Peruvian customs took pity on us and said to Myron, "Tell them, (by phone that is) that customs wants to see them. That will get them here in a hurry!" He did what he was told and in a short while someone arrived and very quickly took us and our baggage by minibus to a hotel in downtown Lima.

At the hotel, all Myron and I could do was drop into bed. We were still so sick when morning arrived that we would gladly have stayed there all day. We had to see what possibilities there were for us getting from Lima to Cochabamba. So, we dressed, tried to eat some breakfast, and then walked to the airline's downtown office. Of course our three lady friends did not speak any Spanish. We were indeed faint, yet pursuing our way to get to our destination. We rejoiced to discover that we were listed on an afternoon flight. After buying some flu medicine, returned to our hotel to tell our friends the good news.

Well, as the saying goes, "All's well that ends well." We had a good flight to Cochabamba and were greeted at the airport by a large group of our fellow-missionaries. We were glad to be back in Bolivia!

Final Days Of Service In Bolivia

❖

Chapter 20

Almost immediately upon our arrival in Cochabamba, Myron was advised that something had to be done about the mission school's land problem. The account of the land problem goes something like this: at the time property was purchased for a school for missionary children, sufficient farm land was also purchased for the raising of vegetables for the school's kitchen. About forty acres in all were purchased. For the first several years we had a good missionary farmer and things went well. There was much work in maintaining the irrigation ditches and cultivating the crops. Consequently, considerable money was also expended on Bolivia labor. In addition, there was the constant problem of trying to keep our neighbor's cows and pigs out of the crops because our farm was located in "open range" country which means all animals roam freely. So, eventually, it was concluded that we could buy our vegetables cheaper from the Bolivia farmers than we could produce them ourselves. In addition, if we purchased our vegetables, a missionary would not be devoting all his time to raising food.

However, since good farm land is scarce in the area of our school, there was considerable ill feeling on the part of our Bolivian neighbors that land suitable for raising crops was sitting idle. In fact we heard that some Quechua Indians were going to come and take it over by force. Finally, we agreed to rent the land to a Bolivian Christian and his brother-in-law, who was also a Christian. It wasn't long before the brother-in-law withdrew from the partnership saying that he found the other fellow incompatible. At first our renter was faithful to pay his rent in either produce or money, but as time went on, he paid nothing and in addition had built houses for both himself and his married son on the property. He had already lost his testimony as a Christian in the community, and in the local church, where he had been a leader. He became belligerent when we tried to deal with him. In fact, at one point, he declared himself a communist and stated that there was a group of university students in the city of Santa Cruz ready to come, at his word, take over by force all of our land.

Two days after our arrival in Bolivia, the Field Chairman and Myron flew from Cochabamba to the city of Santa Cruz, which was the capital of the province in which our school was located. They were told by a lawyer that for the sum of two hundred and fifty dollars we could influence the judge to throw a decision in our favor. But our men decided not to follow our lawyer's advice for two reasons: 1. They didn't like the idea of paying a bribe. 2. They didn't know just what kind of decision would be thrown in our favor. The matter proceeded to higher authorities in the city of La Paz. In order that one might know the outcome of all this, Myron gives an account in brief.

"After several years of litigation and the expenditure of several hundreds of dollars in legal fees, a decision was made by the government in the mission's favor. In spite of all this, we had to pay the renter a couple of thousand dollars to get him off our land which he had been using free of charge. Was this a decision in our favor? At any rate, we didn't lose our property altogether. In addition, this man has since repented of his deeds and has been restored to fellowship in the church." He remains to this day a good friend of our family. He never has, however, made restitution for the money he extracted from the school. I suppose like many others, he thought we "rich Americans" had it to spare.

Once back at Tambo, there was the usual job of reestablishing a household, cleaning a dorm and office, and getting the bookkeeping and other work caught up before the fall term began. After this was done, however, we managed a trip by plane to the remote village of San Buenaventura where Dave and Ruth had gone to work.

Our plane landed at a larger village on the opposite side of the huge Beni River which is a tributary of the mighty Amazon. Dave and Ruth met us at the airport and accompanied us and our baggage on the back of a rickety old truck to the river at which point we and our baggage were placed in a long dugout canoe. David and a Bolivian fellow, both standing up in the canoe, rowed us to the other side. The wind was sweeping down from the Andes Mountains and our ride was just a little scary since the top of the canoe was just a couple of inches above the water. Things were going well with Dave and Ruth except that they were a little concerned for their safety, because there were guerrillas in their area and two German technicians had recently been kidnapped by them. Before our visit with them ended, word was received that all danger had passed. After a good visit with Dave and Ruth, seeing first hand the work that God was doing through them there, we once again returned to Tambo.

There were serious preparations to be made for the classes we were to teach. Our first staff meeting for the semester was also held to finalize preparations for the new school term.

At about this time, we learned that our boat baggage had arrived safely in Cochabamba and had been released without excessive customs fees. Later, enroute to Tambo, the truck on which it was being hauled, overturned and several items were broken. In addition, as we unpacked our boxes we discovered that one-half of all the new curtains a ladies' group had made for our dorm and another dorm had been stolen. As the Lord's servants, we learn to take the spoiling of our goods joyfully, and although it was a disappointment, we knew the Lord makes no mistakes, even in this loss. We prayed that in all of this His name would be glorified.

Although activities in the school were much the same as previous years we had served in Tambo, yet, in a sense, things are different each year because there are always changes in students and sometimes in staff as well.

As to changes in the student body that fall, I think especially of a 12th grade girl who was new to the school and whom we very reluctantly accepted as a student. The reasons were: 1. She was from a Mission that differed considerably from us in doctrinal beliefs. 2. She had had an improper involvement with a Bolivian boy. Her parents were desirous of placing her in a school that was located some distance from the boy's home. The problems we anticipated materialized and some others as well. The girl was not walking with the Lord when she entered the school. In addition, her boyfriend later showed up in the company of another fellow. The whole situation gave us considerable concern, not only for this one girl, but all the girls of our school. Happily, I was able to talk with her and counsel her, and we spent time praying together. She eventually saw the wisdom of mending her ways and she continued with us until her family returned to the United States. There were people rather new on our staff that fall too, and, of course, Myron was new in his position as Chairman of the school. This meant adjustments on the part of everyone. Whenever you have fifteen or more human beings working and living close together you have the potential of fifteen problems. We had a few that semester but we sought to work them out in a Christ-like spirit. All in all, we thanked the Lord for the helpfulness and encouragement of fellow staff members while Myron carried the heavy load of responsibility and work.

An incident that occurred that fall, although not connected with the school, affected us as a family. One day we heard through radio communications that our daughter-in-law, Marilyn was having symptoms of appendicitis. A pilot from another mission tried to fly to their remote station in Tobite to bring her out but was driven back by severe headwinds. Thankfully he was able to make the trip the next morning. Before Marilyn arrived at the hospital, however, her appendix had burst and peritonitis had set in. Never-the-less, she recovered nicely after surgery was performed. To help her and Paul during her convalescent period, we cared for their son Tim for a time at the school. That was a blessing and a joy to be able to care for our first grandson.

Myron's health was not good. He was carrying a heavy load of responsibilities as Chairman of the school, teacher, bookkeeper, Sunday school teacher, something of a pastor of a Bolivian church and a member of the Field Committee. As the semester progressed, so did his health problems with severe stomach aches. Finally, just before school closed in December for the Christmas vacation, he was able to get away from the school and go to Cochabamba for what we thought would be a routine checkup. We both had a surprise in store for us. X-rays revealed a duodenal ulcer and following the x-rays Myron began to hemorrhage internally. Although the Bolivian doctor, who was treating him was rather elated that he had discovered what the American doctors had not discovered back in the United States, he rather gravely said to Myron in broken English, "This ulcer is so large and so bad that I doubt that we can cure it without surgery, but if you will obey me, we will try." Myron responded, "I will obey you."

I was summoned immediately to Cochabamba. I had a tiring all night ride in the very back seat of a very rough riding bus. Only because I had nursing abilities was Myron allowed to stay at the Mission home instead of going to the hospital. He was given a blood transfusion. A moment of amusement came when the doctor made a point of explaining that the blood was from someone who was half Bolivian and half German. As it that made any difference to us. We were certain in our hearts that is was because so many folk on the field were praying that the Lord undertook in those trying times. With care, and medication, and much prayer, the bleeding stopped and surgery was not performed.

There was no possibility of Myron returning to Tambo to work so we were given one of the largest guest rooms in the Mission Home. Kind friends moved a bit of our furniture up from the school so that we could be comfortable.

Dave and Ruth, who were away from their post of service because of Ruth's dental problems, were able to help fill the gap at the school until the term ended. They joined us in Cochabamba for Christmas. Myron was thankful to be alive and comfortable, but wasn't too happy with the strict diet he had to adhere to -- especially over Christmas. Plain Jello and plain milk pudding every two hours for two whole weeks! And that at Christmas time! He resolved then, that when the time came that he could eat some meat and other solid foods, he would never complain about food again!

At the end of January, Myron returned for X-rays so that the doctor could see exactly how the healing of the ulcer was progressing. As the doctor studied the picture he exclaimed, "Una maravilla!" "It's a wonder! One cannot see the ulcer now." Myron replied, "Well, a great many people prayed that I would be healed without surgery." "Let's say it was you plus God."

Inasmuch as the doctor said that he should not return to the mission school, it needed to be decided where we could work. For one thing, Myron would have to be in a place where we could get food in keeping with his diet. It was concluded after much prayer that we should stay in the city of Cochabamba where he would continue to serve on the Field Committee and also be the field bookkeeper. I would serve as room hostess at the mission headquarters and also extend nursing care to any missionaries who might come to the city for medical help. A suitable apartment was made ready for us and we went to work.

Life was by no means dull at mission headquarters. With an almost constant flow of people coming and going, there was much to be done. In addition, Myron was often away with other committee members for several days at a time dealing with field business and problems. This, of course, put him behind in the bookkeeping at headquarters. This didn't help his physical condition any and eventually he had a recurrence of his old problem.

One highlight of our stay in Cochabamba was Priscilla's coming to be with us during the summer of 1971. She had written to us about a Jim Stephens whom she was dating, a fellow student at Tennessee Temple College. He seemed to be very devoted to her but she wished to talk things over with us before she committed herself. Through the kindness of a friend in Michigan, and help from us, she was able to make the trip to Bolivia. While in Bolivia she received a tape from Jim in which he fervently declared his love for her. He also said that whether "they listened to the tape or not, I'll be waiting for you at Miami Airport when you return whether your answer is yes or no."

It wasn't long after Priscilla returned to college that she gave him her answer and we received a letter from Jim asking formal permission to marry her. A lot of joking took place amongst us missionaries as to how much dowry we should ask as they did in Bible times. One fellow missionary cautioned me against setting too high a price on my daughter and getting stuck with her as one man did because the suitor didn't want her that bad!

Eventually, the date of the wedding was set, June ninth, 1972. Priscilla wished so much we could be home for the occasion. In the meantime, a dissatisfied, restless spirit had arisen in Myron's own heart concerning his work in Cochabamba. He didn't mind being a bookkeeper because that was a necessary job in the operation of the mission, but he wasn't happy with the thought of being a bookkeeper for the rest of his life.

Once again we spent much time in prayer about these matters, and we also did a bit of corresponding with the vice-chairman of our mission in the States. He immediately asked us not to look outside the Mission for a place of service.

They had a place for us somewhere in the home program although he couldn't tell us the exact place then. Another organization assured us of a place as well, but we preferred to stay with New Tribes Mission with which we had already worked for twenty-three years.

We took up service the following fall at our mission's Bible Institute in Waukesha, Wisconsin. Myron served as business manager and teacher for six years and in our seventh year assumed the chairmanship as well. I served as secretary and receptionist and switch board operator at the main desk. I also helped students find part time employment in the Waukesha area. We were very happy in the ministry there.

Time marches on and our days were filled. It was a time of trial and testing as well as a time of much blessing. We enjoyed our ministry among the students, and such a wonderful staff with whom to work.

For a couple of years of our time there in Waukesha, David and Grace also became part of the staff. David worked with the maintenance crew and Grace worked in the Bookkeeping office. It was a blessing to have them close by. Brett and Shawn were part of their family at that time, and little Tiffany joined the family while they were in Waukesha.

David and Ruth had returned to Bolivia for another term of service.

During the Christmas time of 1975, we received a never-to-be-forgotten gift from the children. It had all started the summer before when Jim and Priscilla and David and Grace got their heads together and sent out a letter to our donors telling them they would like to send us back to Bolivia for a visit. At Christmas time a book entitled, "A Token of Love," was presented to us with the names of so many people who had responded and sent gifts. Our hearts were overwhelmed. Our passports were still up to date, so there weren't too many problems in getting the other necessary papers and vaccinations necessary. That summer of 1976 we were once again on our way back to Bolivia. Six wonderful weeks were spent visiting the many friends and coworkers. We visited the national churches where we had once worked. What a reunion was ours in visiting once again with those dear believers. Six weeks went by altogether too quickly, and it was time to return to our ministry in Waukesha.

At the end of that seventh year, a health problem arose once again and Myron's doctor encouraged us to get away from the stress of the Bible School. God in His faithfulness provided us with a home in Clarksville, Michigan. About two years previously Edna Richardson, a single lady who had been one of our faithful supporters for many years, made us co-owners of her home with the agreement that we would take care of her when she needed it. We once again saw God's faithfulness in going before us and meeting every need. We moved to Clarksville the beginning of the year 1979. Myron was not well, and friends were so good to help out during that time. We were forced to make a big decision and this was to retire from New Tribes Mission because of all these health problems. Don Seiling, who was serving as the cook for the Bible School at that time was released to help drive the big Rider truck. What an encouragement and blessing everyone was during those difficult days.

Even though Myron's health still was not good, he was able to help out in the church in many ways, even serving for a time as interim pastor.

At about the same time the need to help out in Spanish Bible correspondence work was presented to us. It was with the Source of Light Mission. They needed someone fluent in the Spanish language to be able to correct the lessons of Spanish speaking people, and to follow up these lessons with letters of counsel. Some of these people were prisoners. Others lived in Puerto Rico and Mexico and well as in the United States. It seemed the very thing that would bring encouragement to our hearts. We would still be able to serve our Lord and master, even though we were tied pretty much to our home.

As time went on the Lord blessed that ministry. There were over one hundred people who were sending their lessons to us to be corrected. Edna continued in poor health and the Lord took her Home to be with Himself. Just a few weeks after this, we were privileged to care for Myron's sister Frances there in the home which was ours in Clarksville. She was with us until her death in 1981.

Toward the end of 1980, I had a very unexpected minor heart attack and was hospitalized, first in the local hospital and later was moved to the hospital in Grand Rapids.

The day this happened we were expecting company for supper. Myron was also in Grand Rapids doing some calling for the church. What a surprise he received upon arriving home to find that I had been taken to the hospital. After a few weeks of rest, my health improved and I felt much better.

In August of 1981 while Myron was preaching on his last Sunday of preaching as interim pastor, we were at the door greeting the folk as they left the church. God had another surprise package for us.

An envelope was handed to us by one of these dear couples, Andy and Esta Kole. We weren't to have the opportunity to open it until we were home and then what a surprise we had. There was just a note inside that letter stating that they would like to pay our way back to Bolivia for a visit, to be there when our newest grandchild would be born.

After fifteen years of married life, Dave and Ruth were expecting their first little one. He or she was to be an extra special blessing for they had waited so long. The note also said that we were to let them know just how much the passage would be and they would give us a check for the amount. It seemed as if our excitement would overwhelm us. God was doing it again! We were to make still another visit to Bolivia. We didn't get there in time for little Joel's arrival, but when we arrived at the airport in Cochamba, David and Ruth and Joel were waiting for us. Another six wonderful weeks were spent there in Bolivia, and God was faithful in keeping Myron in fairly good health all that time. We began to believe that our "furloughs" from the United States were always to be spent in Bolivia. That was alright with us because our hearts were there too.

We continued to enjoy our home there in Clarksville, but Myron began having more and more physical problems, and was in and out of the hospital. These were difficult days, with many hospital expenses, plus expenses in keeping up the home. Dave and Ruth also came home on furlough again that year and helped us celebrate our fortieth anniversary, just after Myron had gotten home from another hospital visit.

In 1984 after much prayer and consideration with the whole family -- because of the financial circumstances -- we felt we should sell our Clarksville home. It was a very difficult decision at the time, but as we look back now we see God was in it. One cold, rainy fall day we had an auction and many of the household articles were sold. That same day the house was sold. It was a sad day, but the Lord sustained us through it all. Priscilla came up at that time to help us prepare for the sale and took home many articles from the house for Ruth and Dave too. Other things were stored for Paul and Marilyn.

We made the purchase of a new mobile home. We lived for a year in a mobile home park near Clarksville. Then, because of Myron's declining health and in order to be near David and Grace and family, we had our home moved to Rives Junction where they were living. It was also the time Paul and Marilyn were home on furlough with their three children, Tim, Jonathan and Kathy. David and Ruth were also home from Bolivia with Joel.

What a privilege it was to have Christmas all together once again as a complete family. We met at David's and Jim and Priscilla and family also came to Michigan that Christmas. Little did we know that it would be the last time we would be altogether as a family before the Lord would call some of our number Home to be with Himself.

Two weeks after that family reunion, tragedy struck. Paul and Marilyn and the children were living in the Mission Home in Clarksville. One Saturday they had planned a shopping trip as a family to Grand Rapids, Jonathan had been helping a friend of his haul wood on a tractor for a couple of days, and they wanted to work that Saturday again in order to finish the job. He told his Dad and Mom that he felt the Lord wanted him to stay and continue helping his friend. His parents agreed, and so Jonathan didn't go with the family. His friend was driving the tractor when all of a sudden the brakes failed and the tractor tipped over. Although the boys both tried to jump far enough away, Jonathan was pinned under the seat of the tractor. He was killed instantly. He was just 16 years of age. What a shock Paul and Marilyn got when they arrived home to hear the news that Jonathan had gone to be with the Lord. This was a hard blow for all of us. Jonathan had been a tremendous testimony in the Lake Odessa High School. It came as a shock to all. The principal gave a day off to the high schoolers. There were many young people in attendance at the funeral held in Clarksville. Jonathan was laid to rest beside his Aunt Frances in the Clarksville cemetery.

It wasn't many months after that in September of 1986 when the Lord called my dear hubby Home to be with Himself. Myron had suffered much during the last five years with cancer, but had faithfully kept up with the Spanish Bible correspondence work. He sent his last lesson out just the day before he went into a coma. Although Ruth and Paul had returned to Bolivia, they both came home and all the children were with me during that difficult time. He was laid to rest in the Clarksville cemetery lot which Edna had purchased for us. We had a wonderful marriage and forty-three precious years together. We were so well blessed with the family God gave us with four loving, caring children and their families.

I would also like to mention that during our more than twenty years in Bolivia and our work here at home, we often fell short of what we should have been or done and if anything of eternal worth was accomplished it was accomplished by the grace of God working in and through us. All praise and glory be to His Name!

Three months later God showed me He still had work for me to do.

Keeping Busy -- While Waiting

Chapter 21

When we were married in August of 1943 the Lord gave us a promise that we have carried with us. It's found in Psalm 48:14 "For this God is our God forever and ever; he will be our guide even unto death."

The wonderful meaning of this verse was still precious to me. Although He had taken Myron HOME, yet he would still be my guide until such time as He would call me HOME as well.

Our mobile home served me well. It was comfortable and adequate. It was in a country setting and close to David and Grace.

I felt the Lord stirring my heart, however. Should I return to Bolivia? The answer came not too long after Myron was taken. I was approached by the Mission to come to the retirement center in Oviedo, Florida to help in the nursing ministry there. It was a big decision. It would mean that I would be farther away from the family. Also, because Myron had been ill for so long, in my heart I really wasn't ready for more nursing. How faithful and patient the Lord is with each one of us.

Paul and Ruth were both home for the funeral and now were on their way back to the field. I had gathered the family together and shared with them this proposition which had been made to me. When it came time for Paul and Ruth to leave, Paul said to me, "Mom, how would it be if we got an air ticket for you, and together we will go with you to Florida to see what the Lord has there. We will rearrange our tickets for a layover in Sanford and will be with you to talk things over with our committee there." How I did appreciate the advice of my faithful children.

We purchased our tickets and made arrangements for us to fly to Orlando, Florida and were met there by some of the Mission personnel. The care center wasn't quite finished but as Macon Hare took us around, we could see how the Lord was blessing in the building of this facility for our retirees.

I said I would pray about the situation. There was only one two bedroom apartment available at the time. I believe the Lord had His hand in this, to provide a place which my family could still count as "home".

I was only there for a weekend, and then it was time for me to fly back to Detroit and my home in Jackson, Michigan. Paul and Ruth continued on their flight back to Bolivia and to their ministries there. Since this was only a week after the funeral, it was a difficult thing to re-enter my empty home.

One thing I would like to add here is that I told the Lord that I would feel it was His will to make this move if my family were all in agreement.

It was hard for David and Grace to accept any decision such as this, because unknown to me, Myron had asked David to be faithful in caring for his mother.

When I reached home, however, about the first thing David said to me was they they wanted me to know that whatever decision I made, they would be behind me one hundred percent. Was this God's answer to me? I spent much time in prayer during the next few days. I had told Macon that I would write my answer soon after I arrived home. I told him I would come.

The next few weeks were busy ones. Once again I was preparing to move. This time, and alone. It was a big step, and many times my heart almost failed me wondering what was ahead. How faithful the Lord was in those days, bringing verses of assurance to me from His word, that this was the path in which I should walk.

A dear friend of ours for many years, Evy Jacobs, called one evening to say that she and her hubby Paul had talked things over, and that she would be coming for a week or two to help me with the packing. Once again, God's provision and faithfulness in action. The Jacobs were such a blessing at that time.

Little by little boxes were filled, and the final moving day arrived. What a blessing it was too, for Priscilla to fly up from their home in South Carolina to be with me at this time. We made preparations to drive together to Florida.

The Committee at the New Tribes Mission Homes had agreed to bring the big truck they had to Michigan to move my things to Florida. How I did appreciate this. Yes, once again another sign of God's care and provision.

Two fellows from NTM Homes staff came with the truck. Dan Taube and Bob Bowersox arrived in Rives Junction, Michigan at my home to load the truck. It was early Monday morning, just four days before Thanksgiving, just three months after Myron went HOME. The truck was loaded and on it's way to Florida. Priscilla and I spent a little while cleaning up the last minute things in the trailer. Then we also started driving towards Florida. David would be responsible for the sale of the mobile home.

One night was spent on the road with Jim's family. Then we continued on to Columbia, South Carolina, where the Stephens lived. By the time we got there it was Thanksgiving break from school. That weekend the whole Stephens family and I headed in two cars towards Oviedo, Florida. It was such a blessing to have the family with me. We arrived just a couple of days after the truck had arrived.

I found lots to do in those days, but I counted it a blessing to have such faithful staff members with whom to work. Everyone was so considerate and helpful and gave me a wonderful welcome.

Four years after I arrived there in Oviedo, it was necessary for the entire group at NTM Homes to relocate. The new expressway was to come right through our property. The Lord has given a beautiful place here in Sanford, just one mile from our Mission headquarters. It was only a celery field to begin with, but with volunteer help, we now have a beautiful landscaped setting.

I served with the staff for almost seven years. There were some health problems towards the end of that time which led to my decision to retire -- once again.

Now what do we do? There are quite a few retirees of New Tribes Mission here at our retirement center. However, there are no shuffle boards, nor tennis courts, or any gold courts. There is too much to be done. Yes, that's right. There are many ministries in which our folk have an active part as long as health permits. Three different nursing homes are visited weekly. Once a week a group go to the Juvenile Detention Center to counsel and minister to the young people there. Others go to a jail ministry. Others, go in visitation house to house. We find needy people everywhere. There are people who need the Lord wherever we go. The field is white unto harvest. In the morning five days a week we meet together for a short time of devotion and then break into prayer groups to remember needs on all of our fields. The requests are taken from letters from the field. There are also many personal requests for family needs. Sundays our group branches out into several different churches in the area and are used to help out in these areas as the Lord directs. The Lord was also giving me time to write this story of God's faithfulness to His children. This was a burden on my heart since my hubby was taken Home. God has given strength but also wisdom in remembering many of the experiences the Lord allowed us to have there in Bolivia. To God be the glory!

NTM Homes continues to grow. We have known the Lord's blessing. We have many "Royal" winter volunteers who come with their RV's to help out in the work. Some of our missionaries who are still serving on the field will soon be needing a place to stay. As the Lord provides, the work goes ahead. During the winter months with all of this extra help we see the Lord at work. God has been so faithful in providing funds as well, that we may see our community grow. He is so faithful! When our volunteers leave us it feels as if part of family have gone.

We await the time when we will all be together once again in Heaven with those who have gone before; or until our Lord Jesus comes to take to be with Himself, those who have put their trust in Him. I have much for which to praise the Lord in knowing that our own children have come to know Him as Saviour. Many of our grandchildren have also come to know a walk with the Lord. I'm praying that all may one day be brought into the fold.

In the meantime as Myron would say, there is work to be done. There are still fields white unto harvest. All of our fields are needing more help. Our prayer is day by day that others will see the need of men and women lost in sin because they know not the Saviour. We will need younger men and women to take up the slack. There isn't one of our retirees here who wouldn't want to once again return to their place of service on the foreign field if their health permitted.

Dear reader, would you be the one God would have to help fill the gaps? There are lost men and women, boys and girls, who have no opportunity to hear unless someone goes to give them the message of salvation. Will you be that one whom the Lord would have move out to His place of service for Him?

God is not willing that any should perish. Are you? "Ask of me, and I shall give thee the heathen for thine inheritance, and the uttermost parts of the earth for thy possession." Psalm 2:8.

As I bring this story to a close I would like to relate the experience I had on my last visit to Bolivia in 1988. My brother who lives in Canada and was also a widower at that time went with me. Paul and Marilyn took us to visit many of the places in which we had worked, but the one which made the most impression was the visit to what used to be the leper colony. The land had been cleared of all the big trees, and also the buildings, with one exception. The ground was divided into beautiful, flourishing farm lands.

It is this "one exception" I wish to speak of. As we drove into the colony over a much better road than we once had, I could hardly believe I was in the same place. There was no hospital, no buildings that I could see. We drove right into the middle of the property and there was a log fence, encircling a tiny mud hut. This little dwelling was the only thing left that used to be there. When the colony was disbanded, there were about ten patients, considered the worst cases, left there to die. One still lives in this little humble abode. Paul went to the fence and called out, "Rosalina, please come out, you have some visitors." She wasn't about to come, for she knew she wasn't very pleasing to look at. Eventually, however, she came, hobbling out on her two forked sticks which served as crutches. Rosalina has no hands or feet. She took one look at me, then another look, and with tears streaming down her face said, "Oh, Senora Catalina, did you come back to stay?" My heart was broken! Oh how I would have loved to stay. However, as we talked together, she wasn't telling us of how much she was suffering. Oh no, she was praising the Lord for the fact that we had brought the gospel and that she knew the Lord Jesus as her Saviour. She was looking forward to that time when she will have a new body. She thanked me over and over again for coming to tell them about the Lord. What a testimony!

She is cared for by the farmers who give her food and wood for her fire. Someone always brings her water. She still cooks and lives by herself. Her "stove" consists of a small wood fire on the floor of her dwelling. She has the same "bed" made of cactus slats with a few rags for covering. I'm looking forward to being together with Rosalina in heaven. Yes, I would love to go back, but that isn't possible because of health and age.

The following is a poem which expresses my heart.

Chapter 21

Traveling On My Knees

Last night I took a journey
to a land across the seas.
I didn't go by boat or plane,
I traveled on my knees.

I saw so many people there
In deepest depths of sin.
And Jesus told me I should go-
That there were souls to win.

But I said, "Jesus, I can't go
And work with such as these."
He answered quickly. "Yes, you can,
By traveling on your knees."

And so I tried it, knelt in prayer,
Gave up some hours of ease;
I felt the Lord right by my side
While traveling on my knees.

As I prayed on and saw souls saved.
And twisted bodies healed,
I saw God's workers' strength renewed
While laboring in the field.

I said, "Yes, Lord, I have a job,
'Tis Thee I'd ever please,
I'll gladly go and heed Thy call
While traveling on my knees.

~Sandra Goodwin

THE END

To order additional copies of **Faint Yet Pursuing**, complete the information below.

Ship to: (please print)

Name ____________________

Address ____________________

City, State, Zip ____________________

Day phone ____________________

_____ copies of *Faint Yet Pursuing* @ $6.00 each $ _______

Postage and handling @ $2.50 per book $ _______

Florida residents add 7% tax $ _______

Total amount enclosed $ _______

Make checks payable to *K. Joyce Gess*

Send to: K. Joyce Gess
312 Colombia CT • Sanford, FL 32771-7640 • (407) 321-7582

To order additional copies of **Faint Yet Pursuing**, complete the information below.

Ship to: (please print)

Name ____________________

Address ____________________

City, State, Zip ____________________

Day phone ____________________

_____ copies of *Faint Yet Pursuing* @ $6.00 each $ _______

Postage and handling @ $2.50 per book $ _______

Florida residents add 7% tax $ _______

Total amount enclosed $ _______

Make checks payable to *K. Joyce Gess*

Send to: K. Joyce Gess
312 Colombia CT • Sanford, FL 32771-7640 • (407) 321-7582